SOLOMON'S TEMPLE SPIRITUALIZED.

SOLOMON'S TEMPLE

SPIRITUALIZED,

GOSPEL LIGHT FETCHED OUT OF THE TEMPLE
AT JERUSALEM,
TO LET US MORE EASILY INTO THE GLORY
OF NEW TESTAMENT TRUTHS.

BY

JOHN BUNYAN.

'Thou son of man, shew the house to the house of Israel; shew them the form of the house, and the fashion thereof, and the goings out thereof, and the comings in thereof, and all the forms thereof, and all the ordinances thereof, and all the forms thereof, and all the laws thereof,'—Ezekiel 43:10–11.

A PUBLICATION OF

CURIOSMITH

MINNEAPOLIS,
2010.

Published by Curiosmith.
P. O. Box 390293, Minneapolis, Minnesota, 55439.
Internet: curiosmith.com.
E-mail: shopkeeper@curiosmith.com.

Previously printed as: [London: Printed for, and sold by George Larkin, at the Two Swans without Bishopgate, 1688.]

All explanatory footnotes are from the George Offor edition. The in-text Bible references are footnoted in this edition.

ISBN 9781935626022

CONTENTS.

ADVERTISEMENT BY GEORGE OFFOR.

O F all the wonders of the world, the temple of Solomon was beyond comparison the greatest and the most magnificent. It was a type of that temple not made with hands, eternal in the heavens, of that city whose builder and maker is God, and which, at the consummation of all things, shall descend from heaven with gates of pearl and street of pure gold as shining glass, and into which none but the ransomed of the Lord shall enter. Jesus, the Lamb of God, shall be its light and glory and temple; within its walls the Israel of God, with the honour of the Gentiles, shall be brought in a state of infinite purity. No unclean thing will be able to exist in that dazzling and refulgent brightness which will arise from the perfection of holiness in the immediate presence of Jehovah; and of this, as well as of the whole Christian dispensation, the temple of Solomon was a type or figure. It would have been impossible for the united ingenuity of all mankind, or the utmost stretch of human pride, to have devised such a building, or to have conceived the possibility of its erection. The plan, the elevation, the whole arrangement of this gorgeous temple, proceeded from the Divine Architect. He who created the wondrous universe of nature condescended to furnish the plan, the detail, the ornaments, and even the fashion of the utensils of this stately building. 'David gave to Solomon his son the pattern of the porch, and of the houses thereof, and of the treasuries thereof, and of the upper chambers thereof, and of the inner parlours thereof, and of the place of the mercy seat, and the pattern of all that he had BY THE SPIRIT, of the courts of the house of the LORD, and of all the chambers round about, of the treasuries of the house of God, and of the treasuries of the dedicated things.'[1] 'Now, behold I have prepared for the house of the Lord an hundred thousand talents of gold, and a thousand thousand talents of silver; brass and iron without weight, timber and stone also, and all manner of cunning workmen.'[2] And lest his heart should fail before a work so vast,

[1] 1 Chronicles 28:11–12.
[2] 1 Chronicles 22.

'David said to Solomon, Be strong and of good courage, and do it;
fear not, nor be dismayed: for the Lord God, *even* my God, *will be*
with thee; he will not fail thee, nor forsake thee, until thou hast
finished all the work for the service of the house of the Lord.'[1]
Thus furnished with wisdom from above, with materials and with
cunning workmen, and, above all, with the approbation and
protection of his God, Solomon commenced, and eventually
finished, this amazing structure, and fitted it to receive the
sacred implements, all of which, to the minutest particular, had
been made by Moses, 'after their pattern, which was shewed him
in the mount.'[2]

Every part of the building, including the foundation, its altar,
its courts, the holy of holies, all the utensils, and the ark, were
types of that more glorious system which, in the fulness of time,
appeared as the antitype, and perfected the Divine revelation.
The temple becomes therefore an object of our special attention as
a light to guide us while searching into gospel truths.

Under the peculiar aid of Divine guidance and protection, this
sumptuous structure was finished, and most deeply impressive
were the ceremonies on the day of its consecration. Solomon had
made to himself an everlasting name, and it would be natural to
expect that in such a scene of splendid triumph he would have
felt exalted to the proudest height that human nature was
capable of attaining. But Solomon had not only heard of God by
the hearing of the ear, but by internal communion had seen and
conversed with him. He could say with Job, when he had been
restored from the deepest abasement to an elevated position, 'Mine
eye seeth thee, wherefore I abhor *myself*, and repent in dust and
ashes.' Thus, in Solomon's beautiful prayer on the dedication of
this gorgeous temple, he humbly inquires, 'Will God in very deed
dwell with men on the earth? behold, heaven and the heaven of
heavens cannot contain thee; how much less this house that I
have built?'[3] Thus was completed the most perfect, splendid, and
magnificent building that was ever erected by human hands. Still
it was only a type of that infinitely more glorious antitype, the
Christian dispensation. 'Most stately and magnificent is the
fabric of God's house, yielding admirable delight to such whom

---

[1] 1 Chronicles 28:20.
[2] Exodus 25:40.
[3] 2 Chronicles 6:18.

free grace has vouchsafed to give spiritual eyes to discern it; far surpassing the splendour of its ancient type, the temple of Solomon, which was once the wonder of the world.'[1] 'A greater than Solomon is here.' 'The BRANCH he shall build the temple of the Lord'—the more glorious, spiritual, eternal temple.[2]

In a few hundred years after the temple of Solomon was finished, this sumptuous structure was doomed to destruction, like all the fading handiwork of man. Sin enervated the nation which should have protected it; while the immensity of its riches excited the cupidity of a neighbouring royal robber. It was plundered, and then set on fire; the truth of the declaration made by Job upon the perishable works of man was eminently displayed—'For man to labour he is born, and the sons of the burning coal they mount up fluttering.'[3] In a few days the labour of years, aided by unbounded wealth and resources, was reduced to a heap of ashes. And now, after a lapse of about twenty-five centuries, accompanied by John Bunyan, 'a cunning workman,' as our guide, we are enabled to contemplate the account given us of this amazing edifice recorded in the volume of truth, and to compare that utmost perfection of human art, aided from heaven, with the infinitely superior temple in which every Christian is called to worship—to enter by the blood of the everlasting covenant into the holiest of all, the way consecrated by the cross and sufferings of Christ—without the intervention of priest or lordly prelate—without expensive victims to offer as a type of expiation—without limit of time, or space, or place, the poorest and most abject, with the wealthiest—the humbled beggar and the humbled monarch have equal access to the mercy seat, sacrificing those sinful propensities which are the cause of misery, and pleading the Saviour's merits before the eternal Jehovah. Christ has consecrated the way, and we enter into the holiest of all not only without fear, but with solemn joy. The cost of Solomon's temple has been estimated at eight hundred thousand millions of money: if this is true, still how infinitely inferior is that vast sum to the inconceivable cost of the eternal temple, with its myriads of worshippers, for which the Son of God paid the ransom, when he made the atonement for transgression, and built that imperishable

---

[1] Lee's "Solomon's Temple portrayed by Scripture Light." Dedication.
[2] Zechariah 6:12.
[3] Job 5:7, literally translated from the Hebrew.

temple which neither human nor satanic malevolence can ever destroy, and in which every spiritual worshipper will be crowned with an everlasting weight of glory.

While we cannot doubt but that the temple and its services contained many types highly illustrative of the Christian dispensation, incautious attempts to find them may lead to fanciful interpretations which tend to cloud, rather than to elucidate gospel truths. Bunyan very properly warns his readers against giving the reins to their imaginations and indulging in speculations like those fathers, who in every nail, pin, stone, stair, knife, pot, and in almost every feather of a sacrificed bird could discern strange, distinct, and peculiar mysteries.[1] The same remark applies to the Jewish rabbies, who in their Talmud are full of mysterious shadows. From these rabbinical flints some have thought to extract choice mystical oil to supple the wheels of their fancy—to use a homely expression. Such Jewish rabbies and Christian fathers limped and danced upon one learned leg, to the amazement of all beholders, but not to their edification; their lucubrations may amuse those who have patience to read them, but they afford no instruction. Even the learned Samuel Lee, whose work on the temple abounds with valuable information, has strongly tinctured it with pedantry. It is seldom that a more curious jumble is found than in the following paragraph:—'The waxen comb of the ancient figures and typical eels is fully matted and rolled up in shining tapers, to illuminate temple students in finding out the honey that couches in the carcass of the slain Lion of the tribe of Judah.'[2] There is no fear of Bunyan's indulging his readers with the vagaries of the Jewish rabbies or Christian fathers—his converse was limited to the prophets and apostles. His object is to make us familiar with those types exhibited in the temple and alluded to by the inspired writers of the New Testament; to use a Puritan expression, he would enable us to plough with our spiritual Samson's heifer to expound the riddle, and thus discover the dark patterns of heavenly things.[3] Among the many striking objects to which Bunyan directs our wondering eyes, a few should excite our deeper attention while we accompany him in viewing this marvellous temple.

---

[1] Lee's "Solomon's Temple," p. 173.
[2] Ibid. p. 166.
[3] Hebrews 9:23–24.

1. All the materials that were used required preparation. The stones must be quarried, squared, and fitted for the building with many a hard knock and cutting of the chisel. So must you and I, my readers, pass through the newbirth, and be prepared by the Holy Spirit to fit us for the spiritual building composed of living stones; and if not made meet for that building, we shall be eventually found lifting up our eyes in torment.

2. Very solemn is the consideration insisted on by our author— that all sons are servants to assist in building this spiritual edifice, but all servants are not sons to inherit a place in it; an awful thought, that there have been and now are servants employed in the conversion of sinners, and in building up the saints, who never did nor never will worship in that temple. Let us examine ourselves before we enter that dreary abode, to which we are hastening; 'for *there is* no work nor device, nor knowledge, nor wisdom in the grave, whither thou goest.'[1]

3. Are we zealously affected to forward the work, be careful then as to the materials we use, 'living stones' not wood, hay, or stubble. May all our persuasions be constantly used to bring poor thoughtless sinners to repentance but introduce them not as members of that house until you have a scriptural hope that they have passed from death unto life—that they are believers in Jesus, and have brought forth fruit meet for repentance.

4. All the foundation, the superstructure, the furniture, must be according to the written word of the prophets and apostles, Jesus Christ being the chief corner stone. Reject all the inventions of man and all human authority in the worship of God.

5. The temple was so built that the worshippers looked to the west toward the holy of holies. All the superstitions and idolatrous notions of man lead him to turn to the east, to worship the rising sun. 'The heathen made the chief gates of their temples towards the west, that these stupid worshippers, drawing nigh to their blind, deaf, and dumb deities, might have their idols rising upon them out of the east.'[2] The temple as a type, and Christianity as the antitype, run counter to such idolatrous absurdities and folly.

6. Christian, be content with whatever may be your lot, however humble your place in the church and world. Soon will it be

---

[1] Ecclesiastes 9:10.
[2] Lee's "Solomon's Temple," p. 232.

changed for the better. In this world we are working men, and must be content to be clad and fed as such, that we may be fitted for our solemn and joyful change. Soon we shall put on our church-going holiday suit and partake all the dainties of the heavenly feast, the glories of the New Jerusalem. Reader, these are samples of the prominent truths which will occupy your attention, while accompanying Bunyan in your interesting visit to Solomon's Temple. May you richly enjoy your survey of that astonishing building, under so trusty and experienced a guide.

GEO. OFFOR.

TO THE CHRISTIAN READER.

COURTEOUS CHRISTIAN READER,

I HAVE, as thou by this little book mayest see, adventured, at this time, to do my endeavour to show thee something of the gospel-glory of Solomon's temple: that is, of what it, with its utensils, was a type of; and, as such, how instructing it was to our fathers, and also is to us their children. The which, that I might do the more distinctly, I have handled particulars one by one, to the number of threescore and ten; namely, all that of them I could call to mind; because, as I believe, there was not one of them but had its signification, and so something profitable for us to know.

For, though we are not now to worship God in these methods, or by such ordinances, as once the old church did: yet to know their methods, and to understand the nature and signification of their ordinances, when compared with the gospel, may, even now, when themselves, as to what they once enjoined on others, are dead, may minister light to us. And hence the New Testament ministers, as the apostles, made much use of Old Testament language, and ceremonial institutions, as to their signification, to help the faith of the godly in their preaching of the gospel of Christ.

I may say that God did in a manner tie up the church of the Jews to types, figures, and similitudes; I mean, to be butted and bounded[1] by them in all external parts of worship. Yea, not only the Levitical law and temple, but, as it seems to me, the whole land of Canaan, the place of their lot to dwell in, was to them as ceremonial, or a figure. Their land was a type of heaven, their passage over Jordan into it a similitude of our going to heaven by death.[2] The fruit of their land was said to be uncircumcised.[3] As being at their first entrance thither unclean.[4] In which their

---

[1] Legal terms to define the boundaries of an estate, *butted* upon a common or high road or river, and *bounded* by the property of another person.—(OFFOR.)

[2] Hebrews 3:5–10.

[3] Leviticus 19:23.

[4] Exodus 12:15.

land was also a figure of another thing, even as heaven was a type of sin and grace.[1,2]

Again, the very land itself was said to keep Sabbath, and so to rest a holy rest, even then when she lay desolate, and not possessed of those to whom she was given for them to dwell in.[3]

Yea, many of the features of the then church of God were set forth, as in figures and shadows, so by places and things, in that land. 1. In general, she is said to be beautiful as Tirzah, and to be comely as Jerusalem.[4] In particular, her neck is compared to the tower of David, builded for an armoury.[5] Her eyes to the fish-pools of Heshbon, by the gate of Bethrabbim. Her nose is compared to the tower of Lebanon, which looketh towards Damascus.[6] Yea, the hair of her head is compared to a flock of goats, which come up from mount Gilead; and the smell of her garments to the smell of Lebanon.[7]

Nor was this land altogether void of shadows, even of her Lord and Saviour. Hence he says of himself, 'I AM the rose of Sharon, *and* the lily of the valleys.'[8] Also, she, his beloved, saith of him, 'His countenance *is* as Lebanon, excellent as the cedars.'[9] What shall I say? The two cities Sion and Jerusalem, were such as sometimes set forth the two churches, the true and the false, and their seed Isaac and Ishmael.[10]

I might also here show you, that even the gifts and graces of the true church were set forth by the spices, nuts, grapes, and pomegranates, that the land of Canaan brought forth; yea, that hell itself was set forth by the valley of the sons of Hinnom and Tophet, places in this country. Indeed, the whole, in a manner, was a typical and a figurative thing.

But I have, in the ensuing discourse, confined myself to the

---

[1] Heaven is a type of sin and grace. Had there been no sin, we should have been, limited to an earthly paradise; but sin and the grace of a Saviour's purchase opens heaven to our wondering hearts.—(OFFOR.)
[2] Leviticus 6:17; 23:17.
[3] Leviticus 26:34–35.
[4] Song of Solomon 6:4.
[5] Song of Solomon 4:4.
[6] Song of Solomon 7:4.
[7] Song of Solomon 4:1,11.
[8] Song of Solomon 2:1.
[9] Song of Solomon 5:15.
[10] Galatians 4.

temple, that immediate place of God's worship; of whose utensils, in particular, as I have said, I have spoken, though to each
with what brevity I could, for that none of them are without a
spiritual, and so a profitable signification to us. And here we
may behold much of the richness of the wisdom and grace of
God; namely, that he, even in the very place of worship of old,
should ordain visible forms and representations for the worshippers to learn to worship him by; yea, the temple itself was,
as to this, to them a good instruction.

But in my thus saying, I give no encouragement to any now,
to fetch out of their own fancies figures or similitudes to worship
God by. What God provided to be a help to the weakness of his
people of old was one thing, and what they invented without his
commandment was another. For though they had his blessing
when they worshipped him with such types, shadows, and
figures, which he had enjoined on them for that purpose, yet he
sorely punished and plagued them when they would add to
these inventions of their own.[1] Yea, he, in the very act of
instituting their way of worshipping him, forbade their giving,
in any thing, way to their own humours or fancies, and bound
them strictly to the orders of heaven. 'Look,' said God to Moses,
their first great legislator, '*that* thou make all things according
to the pattern showed to thee in the mount.'[2] Nor doth our
apostle but take the same measures, when he saith, 'If any man
think himself to be a prophet, or spiritual, let him acknowledge
that the things that I write unto you are the commandments of
the Lord.'[3]

When Solomon also, was to build this temple for the worship of
God, though he was wiser than all men, yet God neither trusted
to his wisdom nor memory, nor to any immediate dictates from
heaven to him, as to how he would have him build it. No; he was
to receive the whole platform thereof in writing, by the inspira-
tion of God. Nor would God give this platform of the temple, and
of its utensils, immediately to this wise man, lest perhaps by
others his wisdom should be idolized, or that some should object,
that the whole fashion thereof proceeded of his fancy, only he
made pretensions of Divine revelation, as a cover for his doings.

---

[1] Exodus 32:35; 2 Kings 17:16–18; Acts 7:38–43.
[2] Exodus 25:40; Hebrews 8:5.
[3] 1 Corinthians 14:37.

Therefore, I say, not to him, but to his father David, was the whole pattern of it given from heaven, and so by David to Solomon his son, in writing. 'Then David,' says the text, 'gave to Solomon his son the pattern of the porch, and of the houses thereof, and of the treasuries thereof, and of the upper chambers thereof, and of the inner parlours thereof, and of the place of the mercy-seat, and the pattern of all that he had by the spirit, of the courts of the house of the Lord, and of all the chambers round about, of the treasuries of the house of God, and of the treasuries of the dedicated things: also for the courses of the priests and the Levites, and for all the work of the service of the house of the Lord, and for all the vessels of service in the house of the Lord.'[1]

Yea, moreover, he had from heaven, or by Divine revelation, what the candlesticks must be made of, and also how much was to go to each; the same order and commandment he also gave for the making of the tables, flesh-hooks, cups, basons, altar of incense, with the pattern for the chariot of the cherubims, etc.[2] 'All *this, said David,* the Lord made me understand in writing by *his* hand upon me, *even* all the work of this pattern.'[3] So, I say, he gave David the pattern of the temple, so David gave Solomon the pattern of the temple; and according to that pattern did Solomon build the temple, and no otherwise.

True, all these were but figures, patterns, and shadows of things in the heavens, and not the very image of the things; but, as was said afore, if God was so circumspect and exact in these, as not to leave any thing to the dictates of the godly and wisest of men, what! can we suppose he will now admit of the wit and contrivance of men in those things that are, in comparison to them, the heavenly things themselves?[4]

It is also to be concluded, that since those shadows of things in the heavens are already committed by God to sacred story; and since that sacred story is said to be able to make the man of God perfect in all things[5]—it is duty to us to leave off to lean to common understandings, and to inquire and search out by that

---

[1] 1 Chronicles 28:11–13.
[2] 1 Chronicles 28:14–19.
[3] 1 Chronicles 28:19.
[4] Hebrews 8:5; 9:8–10, 23; 10:1.
[5] 2 Timothy 3:15–17.

very holy writ, and nought else, by what and how we should worship God. David was for inquiring in his temple.[1]

And, although the old church-way of worship is laid aside as to us in New Testament times, yet since those very ordinances were figures of things and methods of worship now; we may, yea, we ought to search out the spiritual meaning of them, because they serve to confirm and illustrate matters to our understandings. Yea, they show us the more exactly how the New and Old Testament, as to the spiritualness of the worship, was as one and the same; only the old was clouded with shadows, but ours is with more open face.

Features to the life, as we say, set out by a picture, do excellently show the skill of the artist. The Old Testament had the shadow, nor have we but the very image; both then are but emblems of what is yet behind. We may find our gospel clouded in their ceremonies, and our spiritual worship set out somewhat by their carnal ordinances.

Now, because, as I said, there lies, as wrapt up in a mantle, much of the glory of our gospel matters in this temple which Solomon builded; therefore I have made, as well as I could, by comparing spiritual things with spiritual, this book upon this subject.

I dare not presume to say that I know I have hit right in every thing; but this I can say, I have endeavoured so to do. True, I have not for these things fished in other men's waters; my Bible and Concordance are my only library in my writings. Wherefore, courteous reader, if thou findest any thing, either in word or matter, that thou shalt judge doth vary from God's truth, let it be counted no man's else but mine. Pray God, also, to pardon my fault. Do thou, also, lovingly pass it by, and receive what thou findest will do thee good.

And for the easier finding of any particular in the book, I have in the leaves following set before thee the chief heads, one by one; and also in what page of the book thou mayest find them. Thy servant in the gospel,

JOHN BUNYAN.

---

[1] Psalm 27:4.

SOLOMON'S TEMPLE SPIRITUALIZED.

I. WHERE THE TEMPLE WAS BUILT.

THE temple was built at Jerusalem, on Mount Moriah, in the threshing-floor of Arnon the Jebusite; whereabout Abraham offered up Isaac; there where David met the angel of the Lord, when he came with his drawn sword in his hand, to cut off the people at Jerusalem, for the sin which David committed in his disorderly numbering the people.[1]

There Abraham received his Isaac from the dead; there the Lord was entreated by David to take away the plague, and to return to Israel again in mercy; from whence, also, David gathered that there God's temple must be built. 'This,' saith he, '*is* the house of the Lord God, and this *is* the altar of the burnt-offering for Israel.'[2]

This Mount Moriah, therefore, was a type of the Son of God, the mountain of the Lord's house, the rock against which the gates of hell cannot prevail.

II. WHO BUILT THE TEMPLE.

THE temple was builded by Solomon, a man peaceable and quiet; and that in name, by nature, and in governing. For so God had before told David, namely, that such a one the builder of the temple should be. 'Behold,' saith he, 'a son shall be born to thee, who shall be a man of rest; and I will give him rest from all his enemies round about; for his name shall be Solomon, and I will give peace and quietness unto Israel in his days. He shall build an house for my name, and he shall be my son, and I *will be* his father.'[3]

As, therefore, Mount Moriah was a type of Christ, as the foundation, so Solomon was a type of him, as the builder of his

[1] Genesis 22:3–5; 1 Chronicles 21:15, 12; 2 Chronicles 3:1.
[2] 1 Chronicles 21:28; 22:1; 3:1.
[3] 1 Chronicles 22:9–10; Psalm 72:1–4.

church. The mount was signal,[1] for that thereon the Lord God, before Abraham and David, did display his mercy. And as Solomon built this temple, so Christ doth build his house; yea, he shall build the everlasting temple, 'and he shall bear the glory.'[2] And in that Solomon was called peaceable, it was to show with what peaceable doctrine and ways Christ's house and church should be built.[3]

III. HOW THE TEMPLE WAS BUILT.

THE temple was built, not merely by the dictates of Solomon, though he was wiser than Ethen, and Heman, and Chalcol, and Darda, and all men.[4] But it was built by rules prescribed by, or in a written word, and as so delivered to him by his father David.

For when David gave to Solomon his son a charge to build the temple of God, with that charge he gave him also the pattern of all in writing; even a pattern of the porch, house, chambers, treasuries, parlours, etc., and of the place for the mercy-seat; which pattern David had of God; nor would God trust his memory with it. 'The Lord made me,' said he, 'understand in writing, by *his* hand upon me, *even* all the works of this pattern.' Thus, therefore, David gave to Solomon his son the pattern of all; and thus Solomon his son built the house of God.[5]

And answerable to this, Christ Jesus, the builder of his own house, WHOSE HOUSE ARE WE, doth build his holy habitation for him to dwell in; even according to the commandment of God the Father. For, saith he, 'I have not spoken of myself, but the Father which sent me. He gave me a commandment what I should speak.' And hence it is said, God gave him the revelation; and again, that he took the book out of the hand of him that sat on the throne; and so acted, as to the building up of his church.[6]

IV. OF WHAT THE TEMPLE WAS BUILT.

THE materials with which the temple was built, were such as were in their own nature common to that which was left behind;

---

[1] One of the types or signs.—(OFFOR.)
[2] Zechariah 6:12–13; Hebrews 3:3–4.
[3] Isaiah 9:6; Micah 4:2–4.
[4] 1 Kings 4:31.
[5] 1 Chronicles 28:9–20.
[6] John 12:49–50; Revelation 1:1; 5:5.

things that naturally were not fit, without art, to be laid on so holy a house. And this shows that those of whom Christ Jesus designs to build his church, are by nature no better than others. But as the trees and stones of which the temple was built, were first hewed and squared before they were fit to be laid in that house, so sinners, of which the church is to be built, must first be fitted by the word and doctrine, and then fitly laid in their place in the church.

For though, as to nature, there is no difference betwixt those made use of to build God's house with, yet by grace they differ from others; even as those trees and stones that are hewed and squared for building, by art are made to differ from those which abide in the wood or pit.

The Lord Jesus, therefore, while he seeketh materials wherewith to build his house, he findeth them the clay of the same lump that he rejecteth and leaves behind. 'Are we better *than they*? No, in no wise.'[1] Nay, I think, if any be best, it is they which are left behind. 'He came not to call the righteous, but sinners to repentance.'[2] And, indeed, in this he doth show both the greatness of his grace and workmanship; his grace in taking such; and his workmanship in that he makes them meet for his holy habitation.[3]

This the current of Scripture maketh manifest; wherefore it is needless now to cite particulars: only we must remember, that none are laid in this building as they come out of the wood or pit, but as they first pass under the hand and rule of this great builder of the temple of God.

V. WHO WAS TO FELL THOSE TREES, AND TO DIG THOSE STONES, WITH WHICH SOLOMON BUILT THE TEMPLE.

As the trees were to be felled, and stones to be digged, so there was for that matter select workmen appointed.

These were not of the sons of Jacob nor of the house of Israel; they were the servants of Hiram, king of Tyre, and the Gibeonites,

---

[1] Romans 3:9.

[2] Mark 2:17.

[3] How universal is this feeling among Christians! 'Why was I made to hear thy voice,' while so many more amiable and less guilty 'make a wretched choice?' All are equally encouraged—'Whosoever will, let him take the water of life freely.'—(OFFOR.)

namely, their children that made a league with Joshua, in the day that God gave the land of Canaan to his people.[1]

And these were types of our gospel ministers, who are the men appointed by Jesus Christ to make sinners, by their preaching, meet for the house of God. Wherefore, as he was famous of old who was strong to lift up his axe upon the thick boughs to square wood for the building of the temple; so a minister of the gospel now is also famous, if much used by Christ for the converting of sinners to himself, that he may build him a temple with them.[2]

But why, may some say, do you make so homely a comparison? I answer, because I believe it is true; for it is grace, not gifts, that makes us sons, and the beloved of God. Gifts make a minister; and as a minister, one is but a servant to hew wood and draw water for the house of my God. Yea, Paul, though a son, yet counted himself not a son but a servant, purely as he was a minister. A servant of God, a servant of Christ, a servant of the church, and your servants for Jesus' sake.[3]

A man then is a son, as he is begotten and born of God to himself, and a servant as he is gifted for work in the house of his Father; and though it is truth the servant may be a son, yet he is not a son because he is a servant. Nor doth it follow, that because all sons may be servants, that therefore all servants are sons; no, all the servants of God are not sons; and therefore when time shall come, he that is only a servant here, shall certainly be put out of the house, even out of that house himself did help to build. 'The servant abideth not in the house for ever,' the servant, that is, he that is only so.[4]

So then, as a son, thou art an Israelite; as a servant, a Gibeonite. The consideration of this made Paul start; he knew that gifts made him not a son.[5]

The sum then is, a man may be a servant and a son; a servant as he is employed by Christ in his house for the good of others; and a son, as he is a partaker of the grace of adoption. But all servants are not sons; and let this be for a caution, and a

---

[1] Joshua 9:22–27; 1 Kings 5:1; 1 Chronicles 28 and 29.
[2] Psalm 7:4–6; Romans 16.
[3] Titus 1:1; Romans 1:1; Colossians 4:5.
[4] Ezekiel 46:16–17; John 8:35.
[5] 1 Corinthians 12:28-31; 13:1–2.

call to ministers, to do all acts of service for God, and in his house with reverence and godly fear; and with all humility let us desire to be partakers ourselves of that grace we preach to others.[1]

This is a great saying, and written perhaps to keep ministers humble: 'And strangers shall stand and feed your flocks, and the sons of the alien *shall be* your ploughmen, and your vine-dressers.'[2] To be a ploughman here is to be a preacher; and to be a vine-dresser here is to be a preacher.[3] And if he does this work willingly, he has a reward; if not, a dispensation of the gospel was committed to him, and that is all.[4]

VI. IN WHAT CONDITION THE TIMBER AND STONES WERE, WHEN BROUGHT TO BE LAID IN THE BUILDING OF THE TEMPLE.

THE timber and stones with which the temple was built, were squared and hewed at the wood or pit; and so there made every way fit for that work, even before they were brought to the place where the house should be set up: 'So that there was neither hammer, nor axe, *nor* any tool of iron heard in the house while it was in building.'[5]

And this shows, as was said before, that the materials of which the house was built were, before the hand of the workman touched them, as unfit to be laid in the building as were those that were left behind; consequently that themselves, none otherwise but by the art of others, were made fit to be laid in this building.

To this our New Testament temple answers. For those of the sons of Adam who are counted worthy to be laid in this building, are not by nature, but by grace, made meet for it; not by their own wisdom, but by the Word of God. Hence he saith, 'I have hewed *them* by the prophets.' And again, ministers are called God's builders and labourers, even as to this work.[6]

No man will lay trees, as they come from the wood, for beams

---

[1] 1 Corinthians 9:25.
[2] Isaiah 61:5.
[3] Luke 9:59–62; 1 Corinthians 9:27; Matthew 20:1–4, 8; 21:28;
    1 Corinthians 9:7.
[4] 1 Corinthians 9:17.
[5] 1 Kings 6:7.
[6] Hosea 6:5; 1 Corinthians 3:10; 2 Corinthians 6:1; Colossians 1:28.

and rafters in his house; nor stones, as digged, in the walls. No; the stones must be hewed and squared, and the trees sawn and made fit, and so be laid in the house. Yea, they must be so sawn, and so squared, that in coupling they may be joined exactly; else the building will not be good, nor the workman have credit of his doings.

Hence our gospel-church, of which the temple was a type, is said to be fitly framed, and that there is a fit supply of every joint for the securing of the whole.[1] As they therefore build like children, that build with wood as it comes from the wood or forest, and with stones as they come from the pit, even so do they who pretend to build God a house of unconverted sinners, unhewed, unsquared, unpolished. Wherefore God's workmen, according to God's advice, prepare their work without, and make it fit for themselves in the field, and afterwards build the house.[2]

Let ministers therefore look to this, and take heed, lest in-stead of making their notions stoop to the Word, they make the Scriptures stoop to their notions.

VII. OF THE FOUNDATION OF THE TEMPLE.

THE foundation of the temple is that upon which it stood; and it was twofold: First, the hill Moriah, and then those great stones upon which it was erected. This hill Moriah, as was said afore, did more properly typify Christ. Hence Moriah is called 'The Mountain of the house,' it being the rock on which it was built. Those great stones, called foundation-stones, were types of the prophets and apostles.[3] Wherefore these stones were stones of the biggest size, stones of eight cubits, and stones of ten cubits.[4]

Now, as the temple had this double foundation, so we must consider it respectively and distinctly; for Christ is the founda-tion one way, the prophets and apostles a foundation another. Christ is the foundation personally and meritoriously; but the prophets and apostles, by doctrine, ministerially. The church then, which is God's New Testament temple, as it is said to be built on Christ the foundation; so none other is the foundation

---

[1] 1 Peter 2:5; Ephesians 2:20–21; 4:16; Colossians 2:19.
[2] Proverbs 24:27.
[3] Matthew 16:18; Ephesians 2:20–21; Hebrews 11:10.
[4] 1 Kings 7:10.

but he.[1] But as it is said to be built upon the apostles, so it is said to have twelve foundations, and must have none but they.[2]

What is it then? Why, we must be builded upon Christ, as he is our priest, sacrifice, prophet, king, and advocate; and upon the other, as they are infallible instructors and preachers of him; not that any may be an apostle that so shall esteem of himself, nor that any other doctrine be administered but what is the doctrine of the twelve; for they are set forth as the chief and last. These are also they, as Moses, which are to look over all the building, and to see that all in this house be done according to the pattern showed to them in the mount.[3]

Let us then keep these distinctions clear, and not put an apostle in the room of Christ, nor Christ in the place of one of those apostles. Let none but Christ be the high-priest and sacrifice for your souls to God; and none but that doctrine which is apostolical, be to you as the mouth of Christ for instruction to prepare you, and to prepare materials for this temple of God, and to build them upon this foundation.

VIII. OF THE RICHNESS OF THE STONES WHICH WERE LAID FOR THE FOUNDATIONS OF THE TEMPLE.

THESE foundation stones, as they were great, so they were costly stones; though, as I said, of themselves, of no more worth than they of their nature that were left behind. Their costliness therefore, lay in those additions which they received from the king's charge.

First, In that labour which was bestowed upon them in saw-ing, squaring, and carving. For the servants, as they were cunning at this work, so they bestowed much of their art and labour upon them, by which they put them into excellent form, and added to their bigness, glory, and beauty, fit for stones upon which so goodly a fabric was to be built.

Secondly, These stones, as they were thus wrought within and without, so, as it seems to me, they were inlaid with other stones more precious than themselves. Inlaid, I say, with stones of divers colours. According as it is written, I 'will lay thy foundations with

---

[1] 1 Corinthians 3:11–12.

[2] Revelation 21:14.

[3] Exodus 39:43; John 20:21–23; 1 Corinthians 3:9; 4:9.

sapphires.'[1] Not that the foundations were sapphires, but they were laid, inlaid with them; or, as he saith in another place, 'They were adorned with goodly stones and gifts.'[2]

This is still more amplified, where it is written of the New Jerusalem, which is still the New Testament church on earth, and so the same in substance with what is now. 'The foundations of the wall of the city,' saith he, '*were* garnished with all manner of precious stones.'[3] True, these there are called 'The foundations of the wall of the city,' but it has respect to the matter in hand; for that which is before called a temple, for its comparative smallness, is here called a city, for or because of its great increase: and both the foundations of the wall of the city, as well as of the temple, are 'the twelve apostles of the Lamb.'[4]

For these carvings and inlayings, with all other beautifications, were types of the extraordinary gifts and graces of the apostles. Hence the apostle calls such gifts signs of apostleship.[5] For as the foundation stones of the temple were thus garnished, so were the apostles beautified with a call, gifts, and graces peculiar to themselves. Hence he says, 'First apostles;' for that they were first and chief in the church of Christ.[6]

Nor were these stones only laid for a foundation for the temple; the great court, the inner court, as also the porch of the temple, had round about them three rows of these stones for their foundation.[7] Signifying, as it seems to me, that the more outward and external part, as well as that more internal worship to be performed to God, should be grounded upon apostolical doctrine and appointments.[8]

IX. WHICH WAY THE FACE OR FRONT OF THE TEMPLE STOOD.

1. The temple was built with its face or front towards the east, and that, perhaps, because the glory of the God of Israel

---

[1] Isaiah 54:11.
[2] Luke 21:5.
[3] Revelation 21:19.
[4] Revelation 21:14.
[5] Romans 15:19; 2 Corinthians 12:12; Hebrews 2:4.
[6] 1 Corinthians 12:28.
[7] 1 Kings 7:12.
[8] 1 Corinthians 3:10–12; 2 Thessalonians 2:15; 3:6; Hebrews 6:1–4.

was to come from the way of the east into it.[1] Wherefore, in that its front stood toward the east, it may be to show that the true gospel church would have its eye to, and expectation from, the Lord. We look, said Paul, but whither? We have 'our conversation,' said he, 'in heaven,' from whence our expectation is.[2]

2. It was set also with its face towards the east, to keep the people of God from committing of idolatry; to wit, from worshipping the host of heaven, and the sun whose rising is from the east. For since the face of the temple stood toward the east, and since the worshippers were to worship at, or with their faces towards the temple, it follows that both in their going to, and worshipping God towards that place, their faces must be from, and their backs towards the sun.[3] The thus building of the temple, therefore, was a snare to idolaters, and a proof of the zeal of those that were the true worshippers; as also to this day the true gospel-instituted worship of Jesus Christ is. Hence he is said, to idolaters, to be a snare and trap, but to the godly a glory.[4]

3. Do but see how God catched the idolatrous Jews, by this means, in their naughtiness: 'And he brought me,' saith the prophet, 'into the inner court of the Lord's house, and behold at the door of the temple of the Lord, between the porch and the altar, *were* about five and twenty men with their backs toward the temple of the Lord, and their faces towards the east.'[5] It was therefore, as I said, set with its face towards the east, to prevent false worship, and detect idolaters.

4. From the east also came the most blasting winds, winds that are destructive to man and beasts, to fruit and trees, and ships at sea.[6] I say, the east wind, or that which comes from thence, is the most hurtful; yet you see, the temple hath set her face against it, to show that the true church cannot be blasted or made turn back by any affliction. It is not east winds, nor none

---

[1] Ezekiel 43:1–4; 47:1.

[2] 2 Corinthians 4:18; Philippians 3:20; Psalms 62:5.

[3] 'To oppose the customs of heathens, who made their chief gates towards the west, that these stupid worshippers, drawing nigh to their blind, deaf, and dumb deities, might have their idols, as it were, arising upon them out of the east.'—(Lee's "Solomon's Temple," p. 242.)—(OFFOR.)

[4] Isaiah 8:14; 60:19.

[5] Ezekiel 8:16.

[6] Exodus 10:13; Job 27:21; Ezekiel 17:10; 19:12; 27:26; Psalm 48:7.

of their blastings, that can make the temple turn about. Hence he saith that Jacob's face shall not wax pale. And again, 'I have made thy face strong against their faces,' and that 'the gates of hell shall not prevail against it.'[1]

5. It might be also built with its face towards the east, to show that the true church looketh, as afore I hinted, for her Lord and King from heaven; knowing, that at his coming he will bring healing in his wings; for from the east he will appear when he comes the second time without sin unto salvation, of which the sun gives us a *memento* in his rising there every morning. 'For as the lightning cometh out of the east, and shineth even unto the west, so shall also the coming of the Son of man be.'[2]

6. Christ, as the north pole, draws those touched with the load-stone of his word, with the face of their souls towards him, to look for, and hasten to his coming. And this also is signified by the temple standing with its face towards the east.

X. OF THE COURTS OF THE TEMPLE.

I PERCEIVE that there were two courts belonging to the temple. The first was called the outward court.[3]

1. This was that into which the people of necessity first entered, when they went to worship in the temple; consequently that was it, in and by which the people did first show their desires to be the worshippers of God. And this answers to those badges and signs of love to religion, that people have in face, or outward appearance.[4]

2. In this, though there may sometimes be truth, yet oftener lies and dissimulation: wherefore commonly an outward appearance is set in opposition to faith and truth, as the outward is in opposition to the inner court, and outward to the inner man; and that is, when it is by itself, for then it profits nothing.[5]

3. Hence, though the outward court was something to the Jews, because by outward bodies they were distinguished from

---

[1] Isaiah 29:22; Ezekiel 3:8; Matthew 16:18.
[2] Matthew 24:27; Malachi 4:2; Hebrews 9:28; Colossians 3:4;
    2 Peter 3:11–14.
[3] Ezekiel 40:7; 46:21.
[4] Matthew 23:27; 2 Corinthians 10:7.
[5] Romans 2:28; 1 Corinthians 13:1–3; 2 Corinthians 5:12.

the Gentiles; yet to us it is little, for now 'he is not a Jew who is one only outwardly.' Therefore all the time of the Beast's reign, this court is given to be trodden under foot; for, as I said, outward show will avail nothing, when the beast comes to turn and toss up professors with his horns.[1]

4. But as there was an outward, so there was an inner court, a court that stood nearer the temple; and so to the true practical part of worship, than that outward court did.[2]

5. This inner court is that which is called 'the court of the priests,' because it was it in which they boiled the trespass-offerings, and in which they prepared the sin-offering for the people.[3]

6. This court, therefore, was the place of practice and of preparation to appear before God, which is the first true token of a sincere and honest mind. Wherefore here, and not in the outward court, stood the great brazen altar, which was a type of Christ, by whom alone the true worshippers make their approach with acceptance unto God. Also here stood the great brazen scaffold, on which the king kneeled when he prayed for the people, a type of Christ's prayers for his when he was in the world.[4]

7. Wherefore this court was a type of practical worship, and so of our praying, hearing, and eating, before God. There belonged to this court several gates, an east, a south, and a north gate; and when the people of the land went into this court to worship, they were not to go out at that gate by which they came in, but out of the gate over against it, to show that true Christians should persevere right on, and not turn back, whatever they meet with in the way. 'He that entereth in by the way of the north gate to worship, shall go out by the way of the south gate; and he that entereth in by the way of the south gate, shall not return by the way of the gate whereby he came in, but shall go forth over against it.'[5]

8. These courts were places of great delight to the Jews, as both feigned and sincere profession is to those that practice

---

[1] Revelation 11:10–12.

[2] Ezekiel 10:3; 46:1; 1 Kings 6:36.

[3] 2 Chronicles 4:9; Ezekiel 46:20.

[4] 2 Chronicles 6:13; John 17.

[5] Ezekiel 46:9.

therein. Wherefore, when the Jews did enter into these, they did use to do it with praise and pipe, as do both hypocrites and sincere ones. So then, when a man shall tread in both these courts, and shall turn what he seems to be, into what he *should* be in reality; then, and not till then, he treads them as he should; for then he makes the outward court, and his treading there but a passage to that which is more inward and sincere. But he that stays in the outward one is but such an one as pleases not God, for that he wants the practice of what he professes with his mouth.

XI. OF THE GREAT BRAZEN ALTAR THAT STOOD IN THE INNER COURT OF THE TEMPLE.

1. In the inner court stood the great brazen altar which Solomon made. This is evident; for that when he kneeled upon the scaffold there to pray, he kneeled before this altar.[1]

2. This altar seems to be placed about the middle of this court over against the porch of the house; and between it and the temple was the place where Zechariah was slain. This altar was called 'the altar of burnt-offering,' and therefore it was a type of Christ in his divinity. For Christ's body was our true burnt-offering, of which the bodies of the sacrificed beasts were a type; now that altar upon which his body was offered was his Divinity or Godhead; for that, and that only, could bear up that offering in the whole of its suffering; and that therefore, and that only, was to receive the fat, the glory. Hence it is said he, 'through the eternal Spirit, offered himself without spot to God.'[2]

3. For Christ is priest, and sacrifice, and altar, and all. And as a priest he offered, as a sacrifice he suffered, and as God he supported his humanity, in that suffering of all the pains it underwent.[3]

4. It was then Christ's Godhead, not the tree, that was the altar of burnt-offering, or that by which Christ offered himself an offering and a sacrifice to God for a sweet-smelling savour.

5. That it was not the tree, is evident, for that could not sanctify the gift, to wit, his body; but Christ affirmeth, 'that the altar sanctifieth the gift.' And by so saying, he affirmeth that the

---

[1] Exodus 40:6, 29; 2 Chronicles 6:13; 2 Kings 16:14; Joel 2:17.
[2] Hebrews 9:14.
[3] Galatians 1:4; 2:20; 1 Peter 3:18; Hebrews 9:14.

altar on which he offered his offering was greater than the offering itself.[1] Now the body of Christ was the gift; for so he saith, I give my flesh for the life of the world.[2]

But now, what thing is that which is greater than his body, save the altar, his Divinity on which it was offered? The tree then was not the altar which sanctified this gift, to make it of virtue enough to make reconciliation for iniquity.[3] Now, since this altar of burnt-offering was thus placed in the inner court, it teaches us several things:

First, That those that come only into the outward court, or that rest in a bare appearance of Christianity, do not, by so doing, come to Jesus Christ; for this altar stands not there. Hence John takes notice only of the temple and this altar, and them that worship therein, and leaves out the outward court, and so them that come no farther.[4]

Second. This teaches us also that we are to enter into that temple of God by blood. The altar, this altar of burnt-offering, stood as men went into the temple; they must go by it; yea, there they must leave their offering, and so go in and worship, even as a token that they came thither by sacrifice and by blood.

Third. Upon this altar Solomon, at the dedication of the temple, offered thousands, both of oxen and of sheep, to signify, surely, the abundant worth and richness that would be in the blood of Christ to save when it should be shed for us. For his blood is spoken of with an 'how much more.' 'For if the blood of bulls and of goats, and the ashes of an heifer sprinkling the unclean, sanctifieth to the purifying of the flesh, how much more shall the blood of Christ, who through the eternal Spirit offered himself without spot to God, purge your conscience from dead works, to serve the living God!'[5]

Let us then not dare to stop or stay in the outward court, for there is not this altar. Nor let us dare, when we come into this court, to be careless whether we look to this altar or no. For it is by blood we must enter; 'for without shedding of blood is no remission.' Let us always then, when we come hither, wash our hands in innocency, and so compass this holy altar: for that by

---

[1] Matthew 23:19.
[2] John 6.
[3] John 6:51; 17:19; Hebrews 9:14; Colossians 1:19–21.
[4] Revelation 11:1–2.
[5] Hebrews 9:13–14; 11:12; 2 Chronicles 7:5–8.

Christ, who is the altar indeed, we are reconciled to God. This is looking to Jesus; this is coming to God by him, of whom this altar and the sacrifice thereon was a type.

XII. OF THE PILLARS THAT WERE BEFORE THE PORCH OF THE TEMPLE.

THERE were divers pillars belonging to the temple; but in this place we are confined to speak of only two; namely, those which stood before the temple.

These pillars stood before the porch or entrance into the temple, looking towards the altar, the court, and them that were the worshippers there; also they were a grace and beauty to the front of the house.

1. These pillars stood, one on the right hand and the other on the left, at the door of the porch of the temple, and they had names given them, you may be sure, to signify something. The name of that on the right hand was called *Jachin*, he [God] shall establish; and the name of that on the left hand was *Boaz*, in it is strength.[1]

2. These two pillars were types of Christ's apostles; of the apostles of circumcision, and of the uncircumcision. Therefore the apostle Paul also calleth them pillars,[2] and saith that that pillar on the right hand was a type of himself and his companions, who were to go to the uncircumcised, and teach the Gentiles the way of life. When James, Cephas, and John, saith he, 'who seemed to be pillars, perceived the grace that was given unto me, they gave to me and Barnabas the right hand of fellowship, that we *should go* unto the heathen, and they unto the circumcision.'[3] So then, these two pillars were types of these two orders of the apostles in this their divers service for God.[4]

3. And that Paul and Barnabas were signified by those on the right hand, to wit, to be the apostles of the Gentiles, he showeth again, where he saith, I am 'the minister of Jesus Christ to the Gentiles, ministering the gospel of God, that the offering up of

---

[1] 1 Kings 7:21; 2 Chronicles 3:17.

[2] Galatians 2.

[3] Galatians 2:9.

[4] 'There were two pillars, which some resemble to the two states of the church—Jewish and Christian; others understand magistracy and ministry.'—(Lee's "Temple," 1659, p. 281.)—(OFFOR.)

the Gentiles might be acceptable, being sanctified by the Holy Ghost.'[1]

4. And since the name of this pillar was *Jachin*, God shall establish, as it showeth that opposition shall attend it; so also, that God would bless his word preached by them to the Gentiles, to the conversion of numbers of them, maugre the opposition of the enemy.

5. This is further implied, for that they were made of brass; as he saith of the prophet, I have made thee a fenced brazen wall, an iron pillar; and their fighting against thee shall nothing at all prevail.[2] Wherefore Paul says of himself, 'I am set for the defence of the gospel,' 'that the truth thereof might continue with you.'[3]

XIII. OF THE HEIGHT OF THESE PILLARS THAT THUS STOOD BEFORE THE PORCH OF THE DOOR OF THE TEMPLE.

THE pillars were eighteen cubits high a-piece, and that is as high, yea, as high again as the highest giant that ever we read of in the Word; for the highest of which we read was but six cubits and a span. True, the bedstead of Og was nine cubits long, but I trow the giant himself was shorter.[4,5] But put the longest to the longest, and set the one upon the shoulders of the other, and yet each pillar was higher than they.

We have now, as I know of, but few that remain of the remnant of the giants; and though they boast as if they were higher than Agag, yet these pillars are higher than they. These pillars are the highest; you may equal them; and an inch above is worth an ell below. The height therefore of these pillars is, to show us what high dignity God did put upon those of his saints whom he did call to be apostles of the Lamb: for their office and call thereto is the

---

[1] Romans 11:13; 15:16.

[2] Jeremiah 15:20.

[3] Philippians 1:17; Galatians 2:5.

[4] Deuteronomy 3:11; 2 Chronicles 3:15.

[5] The height of these pillars was thirty-five cubits each, including the base and chapiter. The base, ornamented with lines or network, twelve cubits; the column eighteen cubits, and the chapiter five cubits, making the height thirty-five cubits; while the column or pillar, cast by itself, was only eighteen. This reconciles the apparent discrepancy between 1 Kings 7:15 and 2 Chronicles 3:15.—(OFFOR.)

highest in the church of God. These men, I say, were made thus high by their being cast in such a mould. Of that which added yet further to their height we will speak anon: we only speak now of the high call by which they, and only they, were made capable of apostolic authority. The apostles were sent immediately,[1] their call was extraordinary, their office was universal; they had alike power in all churches, and their doctrine was infallible.[2]

And what can our pretended giants do or say in comparison of these? The truth is, all other men to these are dwarfs, are low, dark, weak, and beneath, not only as to call and office, but also as to gifts and grace. This sentence, 'Paul, an apostle of Jesus Christ,' drowneth all! What now are all other titles of grandeur and greatness, when compared with this one sentence?

True, the men were but mean in themselves; for what is Paul or what Apollos, or what was James or John? Yet by their call to that office they were made highest of all in the church. Christ did raise them eighteen cubits high; not in conceit; for so there are many higher than they, but in office, and calling, and Divine authority.

And observe it, these stand at the door, at the entering into the temple of God, at which they enter that go in thither to worship God, to shew that all right worship, and that which will be acceptable to God, is by, or according to, their doctrine.

XIV. OF THE CHAPITERS (CAPITALS) OF THE PILLARS OF THE TEMPLE.

THERE were also two chapiters made for the pillars of the temple; for each, one; and they were five cubits high apiece. These were for the adorning of the pillars, and therefore were types and shadows of that abundance of grace which God did put upon the apostles after the resurrection of our Lord. Wherefore, as he saith here, the chapiters were upon the pillars; so it saith that great grace was upon all the apostles.[3]

These chapiters had belonging to them a bowl made pummil-fashion,[4] and it was placed upon the head of them, perhaps to

---

[1] Immediately, or by Christ himself.—(OFFOR.)
[2] Acts 26:16; 1 Corinthians 9:1; Galatians 1:1; 1 John 1:1–3; John 2:23.
[3] Acts 4:33.
[4] Pummil, or pommel, round like an apple.—(OFFOR.)

signify their aptness to receive, and largeness to contain of the dew of heaven; that shadow of the doctrine of the gospel; which doctrine the apostles, as the chief, were to receive and hold forth to the world for their conversion. Hence, as the bowls were capable to receive the dew of heaven, these are said to receive 'grace and apostleship for obedience to the faith among all nations, for his name.'[1]

There was also upon these chapters a net-work, or nets like unto chequer-work, which still added to their lustre. These nets were they which shewed for what intent the apostolical office was ordained; namely, that by their preaching they might bring many souls to God. And hence Christ calls them fishermen, saying, 'Ye shall catch men.'[2] The world is compared to a sea, men to fishes, and the gospel to a net.[3] As therefore men catch fish with a net, so the apostles caught men by their word, which word, as I told you, to me is signified by this net-work upon the top of these pillars. See therefore the mystery of God in these things.

XV. OF THE POMEGRANATES ADJOINED TO THESE NETS ON THE CHAPITERS.

THERE were also joined to these nets upon the top of the pillars pomegranates in abundance; four hundred for the net-work. Pomegranates, you know, are beautiful to look on, pleasant to the palate, comfortable to the stomach, and cheering by their juice.[4] There were to be two rows of these pomegranates for one net-work, and so two rows of them for the other.

And this was to show that the net of the gospel is not an empty thing; but is sufficiently baited with such varieties as are apt to allure the world to be catched by them. The law is but a sound of words, but the gospel is not so; that is, baited with pomegranates; with variety of excellent things. Hence it is called 'the gospel of the kingdom,' and 'the gospel of the grace of God,' because it is, as it were, baited with grace and glory, that sinners may be allured, and may be taken with it to their eternal salvation.[5]

---

[1] Romans 1:5; 1 Kings 7:16, 42; 2 Chronicles 4:13; Deuteronomy 32:10; Romans 15:29.

[2] Matthew 4:19; Mark 1:17; Luke 5:10; 2 Corinthians 12:16.

[3] Ezekiel 47:10–12; Matthew 13:47–50.

[4] 1 Kings 7:42; Song of Solomon 4:3; 8:2; 4:13; 6:11; 7:12.

[5] Matthew 24:14; Acts 20:24.

Grace and glory, grace and glory! these are the pomegranates with which the word of the gospel is baited, that sinners may be taken and saved thereby. The argument of old was 'milk and honey;' that was, I say, the alluring bait, with which Moses drew six hundred thousand out of Egypt, into the wilderness of old.[1] But behold we have pomegranates, two rows of pomegranates; grace and a kingdom, as the bait of the holy gospel; no wonder, then, if, when men of skill did cast this net into the sea, such numbers of fish have been catched, even by one sermon.[2] They baited their nets with *taking* things, things taking to the eye and taste.

Nets are truly instruments of death, but the net of the gospel doth catch to draw from death; wherefore this net is contrary; life and immortality is brought to light through this. No marvel, then, if men are so glad, and that for gladness they leap like fishes in a net, when they see themselves catched in this drag of the holy gospel of the Son of God. They are catched from death and hell, catched to live with God in glory!

XVI. OF THE CHAINS THAT WERE UPON THESE PILLARS THAT STOOD BEFORE THE TEMPLE.

As there were nets to catch, and pomegranates to bait, so there were chains belonging to these chapiters on these pillars. 'And he made chains, *as* in the oracle, and put *them* upon the head of the [pillars],' or chapiters.[3]

But what were these chains a type of? I answer, they were, perhaps, a type of those bonds which attend the gospel, by which souls taken are tied fast to the horns of the altar. Gospel grace, and gospel obligations, are ties and binding things; they can hold those that are entangled by the word. 'Love *is* strong as death;' bands of love, and the cords of a man, and chains take hold on them that are taken by the gospel.[4]

But this strength to bind lieth not in outward force, but in a sweet constraint, by virtue of the displays of undeserved love. 'The love of Christ constraineth us.'[5] Wherefore as you find the

---

[1] Exodus 3:8.
[2] Acts 2.
[3] 2 Chronicles 3:16.
[4] Hosea 11; Song of Solomon 8:6.
[5] 2 Corinthians 5:14.

nets, so the chains had pomegranates on them. 'And' he 'made an hundred pomegranates, and put *them* upon the chains.'[1] The chains then had baits, as well as the nets, to show that the bands of the gospel are unresistible goodnesses; such with which men love to be bound, and such as they pray they may be held fast by. He binds his foal to the vine; his saint unto this Saviour.[2]

By these chains there is therefore showed what strength there is in gospel-charms, if once the adder doth but hear them. Never man yet was able to resist them that well did know the meaning of them. They are mighty to make poor men obedient, and that in word and deed. These chains were such as were in the oracle, to show that gospel bonds are strong as the joys of heaven, and as the glories there; can make them chains as in the oracle, as in the most holy place. It is heaven that binds sinners on earth to the faith and hope of the gospel of Christ.

XVII. OF THE LILY WORK WHICH WAS UPON THE CHAPITERS, THAT WERE UPON THESE PILLARS OF THE TEMPLE.

THESE pillars were also adorned with lily work, as well as with pomegranates and chains. 'The chapiters that were upon the top of the pillars *were* of lily work;' 'so was the work of the pillars finished.'[3]

This lily work is here put in on purpose, even to show us how far off those that were to be the true apostles of the Lamb should be from seeking carnal things, or of making their prevailing[4] a stalking-horse to worldly greatness, and that preferment. There was lily work upon them; that is, they lived upon the bounty and care of God, and were content with that glory which he had put upon them. 'The lilies,' saith Christ, 'they toil not, neither do they spin, and yet ... Solomon in all his glory was not arrayed like one of these.'[5] Thus, therefore, these pillars show, that as the apostles should be fitted and qualified for their work, they should be also freed from cares and worldly cumber; they should be content with

---

[1] 2 Chronicles 3:16.

[2] Genesis 49:11.

[3] 1 Kings 7:19–22.

[4] In all the editions of this book published since the author's death, these words are altered to 'their preaching.'—(OFFOR.)

[5] Matthew 6:28–29; Luke 12: 27–29.

God's providing for them, even as the goodly lilies are. And as thus prepared, they were set in the front of the house, for all ministers to see and learn, and take example of them how to behave themselves as to this world in the performing of their office.

And that which gives us further light in this is, that this lily work is said, by divine institution, to be placed 'over against the belly,' the belly of the pillars, a type of ours.[1] The belly is a craving thing; and these things, saith the text, were placed over against the belly, to teach that they should not humour, but put check unto the havings and cravings of the belly; or to show that they need not do it, for that he that calls to his work will himself provide for the belly. It is said of the church, that 'her belly is like a heap of wheat set about with lilies.'[2] To show that she should without covetousness have sufficient, if she would cast all her care upon God, her great provider. This the apostles did, and this is their glory to this day.

'So was the work of the pillars finished.' To live lily lives, it seems, is the glory of an apostle, and the completing of their office and service for God. But this directly opposite to the belly, over against the belly, and this makes it the harder work. But yet, so living is the way to make all that is done sweet-scented, to those that be under this care. Covetousness makes a minister smell frowish,[3] and look more like a greedy dog, than an apostle of Jesus Christ. Judas had none of this lily work; so his name stinks to this day. 'He that grows like the lily shall cast forth his scent like Lebanon, his branches shall spread, and his beauty shall be as the olive tree, and his smell as Lebanon.'[4] Thus lived Christ, first; and thus the apostles, next; nor can any other as to this, live like, or be compared to them. They coveted no man's silver or gold, or apparel. They lived like lilies in the world, and did send forth their scent as Lebanon.

Thus you see of whom these pillars were a shadow, and what their height, their chapiters, their bowls, their nets, their chains, their pomegranates, and their lily work did signify, and how all was most sweetly answered in the antitype. These were

---

[1] 1 Kings 7:20.

[2] Song of Solomon 7:2.

[3] Frowish, or frowzy, fetid, musty. Alas! how many ministers there are who are afflicted with this unsavoury smell.—(OFFOR.)

[4] Hosea 14:6.

men of the first rate; the apostles, I mean, were such.

XVIII. OF THE FASHION OF THE TEMPLE.

OF the length and breadth of the temple I shall say nothing; but as to the height thereof, there methinks I see something. The temple was higher than the pillars, and so is the church than her officers; I say, consider them singly as officers, though inferior as to gifts and office; for, as I said before of ministers in general, so now I say the same of the apostles, though as to office they were the highest, yet the temple is above them. Gifts and office make no men sons of God; as so, they are but servants, though these were servants of the highest form. It is the church, as such, that is the lady, a queen, the bride, the Lamb's wife; and prophets, apostles, and ministers, etc., are but servants, stewards, labourers for her good.[1] As therefore the lady is above the servant, the queen above the steward, or the wife above all her husband's officers, so is the church, as such, above these officers. The temple was higher than the pillars.

Again, as the temple was highest, so it enlarged itself still upward; for as it ascended in height, so it still was wider and wider; even from the lowest chambers to the top.

The first chambers were but five cubits broad, the middle ones were six, but the highest were seven cubits.[2] The temple therefore was round about above some cubits wider than it was below; for '*there was* an enlarging and winding about still upward to the side chambers, for the winding about . . . went still upward round about the house; therefore the breadth of the house *was still* upward, and so increased *from* the lowest *chamber* to the highest, by the midst.'[3]

And this was to show us that God's true gospel temple, which is his church, should have its enlargedness of heart still upward, or most for spiritual and eternal things: wherefore he saith, 'Thy heart shall fear and be enlarged,' that is, be most affected with things above, 'where Christ sitteth on the right hand of God.'[4] Indeed it is the nature of grace to enlarge itself still upward,

---

[1] Psalm 45:9; Revelation 19:7; 1 Corinthians 3:5; 4:1–2.
[2] 1 Kings 6:5–6.
[3] Ezekiel 41:7.
[4] Isaiah 60:5; Colossians 3:1.

and to make the heart widest for the things that are above. The temple therefore was narrowest downwards, to show that a little of earth, or this world, should serve the church of God. And having food and raiment, let us be therewith content.

But now, upwards, and as to heavenly things, we are com-manded to be covetous, as to them, and after them to enlarge ourselves, both by the fashion of the temple, as by express words.[1]

Since, then, the temple was widest upward, let us imitate it, and have our conversation in heaven. Let our eyes, our ears, our hands, and hearts, our prayers, and groans, be most for things above. Let us open our mouths, as the ground that is chapt doth for the latter rain, for the things that are eternal.[2]

Observe again, that the lowest parts of the temple were the narrowest part of the temple; so those in the church who are nearest, or most concerned with earth, are the most narrow-spirited as to the things of God. But now let even such a one be taken up higher, to above, to the uppermost parts of the temple, and there he will be enlarged, and have his heart stretched out. For the temple, you see, was widest upwards; the higher, the more it is enlarged. Paul being once caught up into paradise, could not but be there enlarged.[3]

One may say of the fashion of the temple, as some say of a lively picture, it speaks. I say, its form and fashion speaks; it says to all saints, to all the churches of Christ, open your hearts for heaven, be ye enlarged upwards!

I read not in Scripture of any house, but this that was thus enlarged upwards; nor is there anywhere, save only in the church of God, that which doth answer this similitude. All other are widest downward, and have the largest heart for earthly things. The church only is widest upward, and has its greatest enlargements towards heaven.

XIX. OF THE OUTWARD GLORY OF THE TEMPLE.

I DO also think, that as to this, there was a great expression in it; I mean, a voice of God, a voice that teacheth the New Testa-ment church to carry even conviction in her outward usages

---

[1] 1 Kings 4:29; Isaiah 60:5; Philippians 3:14; 1 Corinthians 12:31;
    1 Timothy 6:8; Psalm 119:32.
[2] Job 29:23; Psalm 81:10.
[3] 2 Corinthians 12.

that, I say, might give conviction to the world. And besides this of its enlarging upwards, there was such an outward beauty and glory put upon it, as was alluring to beholders. The stones were curiously carved, and excellently joined together; its outward show was white and glittering, to the dazzling of the eyes of the beholders; yea, the disciples themselves were taken with it, it was so admirable to behold. Hence it is said, they came to Christ to show him the building of the temple. 'Master,' said they, 'see what manner of stones, and what buildings *are here*.'[1] And hence it is said, that kings, and the mighty of the earth, were taken with the glory of it. 'Because of thy temple at Jerusalem, shall kings bring presents unto thee;' as it is.[2]

Kings, Gentile kings, they shall be so taken with the sight of the outward glory of it; for they were not suffered to go into it; no uncircumcised were admitted in thither. It was therefore the outward glory of it with which the beholders were thus taken.

Her enlarging upward, as that was to show us what the inward affections of Christians should be, so her curious outward adorning and beauty was a figure of the beauteous and holy conversation of the godly.[3] And it is brave, when the world are made to say of the lives and conversations of saints, as they were made to say of the stones and outward building of the temple, Behold, what Christians, and what goodly conversations are here! I say it is brave when our light so shines before men, that they seeing our good works shall be forced to glorify our Father which is in heaven.[4]

Hence this is called our adorning wherewith we adorn the gospel, and that by which we beautify it.[5] This, I say, is taking to beholders, as was this goodly outside of the temple. And without this, what is to be seen in the church of God? Her inside cannot be seen by the world, but her outside may. Now, her outside is very homely, and without all beauty, save that of the holy life; this only is her visible goodliness. This puts to silence the ignorance of foolish men. This allureth others to fall in love with their own salvation, and makes them fall in with Christ against the devil and his kingdom.

---

[1] Matthew 24:1; Mark 13:1; Luke 21:5.
[2] Psalm 68:29, 31.
[3] Colossians 3:1–3.
[4] Matthew 5:16.
[5] Titus 2:10.

XX. OF THE PORCH OF THE TEMPLE.

WE come next to the porch of the temple that is commonly called
Solomon's. 1. This porch was in the front of the house, and so
became the common way into the temple.[1] 2. This porch therefore was the place of reception in common for all, whether Jews
or religious proselytes, who came to Jerusalem to worship.[2] 3.
This porch had a door or gate belonging to it, but such as was
seldom shut, except in declining times, or when men put themselves into a rage against those better than themselves.[3] 4. This
gate of this porch was called Beautiful, even the Beautiful gate
of the temple, and was that at which the lame man lay, to beg
for an alms of them that went in thither to worship.[4]

Now then, since this porch was the common place of reception
for all worshippers, and the place also where they laid the beggars, it looks as if it were to be a type of the church's bosom for
charity. Here the proselytes were entertained, here the beggars
were relieved, and received alms. These gates were seldom shut;
and the houses of Christian compassion should be always open.
This therefore beautified this gate, as charity beautifies any of
the churches. Largeness of heart, and tender compassion at the
church-door, is excellent; it is the bond of perfectness.[5]

The church-porch to this day is a coming in for beggars, and
perhaps this practice at first was borrowed from the beggars
lying at the temple-gate. This porch was large, and so should the
charity of the churches be. It was for length the breadth of the
temple, and of the same size with 'the Holiest of all.'[6] The first
might be to teach us in charity we should not be niggardly, but,
according to the breadth of our ability, we should extend it to all
the house; and that in our so doing, the very emblem of heaven
is upon us, of which the holiest was a figure. 'As we have therefore opportunity, let us do good unto all,' etc.[7]

It is a fine ornament to a true church to have a large church-
porch, or a wide bosom, for reception of all that come thither to

---

[1] 1 Kings 6:3; 2 Chronicles 3:4.

[2] Acts 3:11; 5:12.

[3] 2 Chronicles 29:7; Acts 21:28–30.

[4] Acts 3:1–2, 10.

[5] 1 Corinthians 12:31; 13:1–4; Hebrews 13:1–3; John 5:6–7;
Colossians 3:14.

[6] 1 Kings 6:3; 2 Chronicles 3:4.

[7] Galatians 6:10.

worship.[1] This was commanded to the Jews, and their glory shone when they did accordingly: 'And it shall come to pass, *that* in what tribe the stranger sojourneth, there shall ye give *him* his inheritance, saith the Lord God.'[2]

This porch was, as I said, not only for length the breadth of the temple, and so the length and breadth of the holiest; but it was, if I mistake not, for height far higher than them both: for the holy place was but thirty cubits high, and the most holy but twenty; but the porch was in height an hundred and twenty cubits. This beautiful porch, therefore, was four times as high as was the [oracle in] temple itself.[3]

One excellent ornament, therefore, of this temple was, for that it had a porch so high, that is, so famous for height; hence he says, 'This house that is so high,' that is so famous for height. So high as to be seen afar off. Charity, if it be rich, runs up from the church like a steeple, and will be seen afar off; I say, if it be rich, large, and abounds. Christ's charity was blazed abroad; it was so high no man could hide it: and the charity of the churches will be seen from church to church, yea, and will be spoken of to their commendations in every place, if it be warm, fervent, and high.[4]

XXI. OF THE ORNAMENTS
OF THE PORCH OF THE TEMPLE.

THERE were three things belonging to the porch, besides its height, that were ornaments unto it. 1. It was overlaid within with gold. 2. It had the pillars adjoined unto it. 3. It was the inlet into the temple.

First. It was overlaid with gold. Gold ofttimes was a type of grace, and particularly of the grace of love. That in Solomon's chariot called gold is yet again mentioned by the name love.[5] As

---

[1] This is a valuable lesson to the ministers and members of churches, to be ever ready to welcome the returning prodigal. The porch is never to be shut against the poor fugitive; and the only proper inquiry as to opening the door of the church, is, 'If thou believest with all thine heart, thou mayest freely enter.'—(OFFOR.)

[2] Ezekiel 47:23.

[3] 1 Kings 6:2, 20; 2 Chronicles 3:4.

[4] Mark 7:36–44; 2 Corinthians 8:24; 9:2; 9:13–14.

[5] Song of Solomon 3:9–10.

it is in the church, the grace of love is as gold. It is the greatest, the richest of graces, and that which abides for ever. Hence they that show much love to saints are said to be rich.[1] And hence charity is called a treasure, a treasure in the heavens.[2] Love is a golden grace; let then the churches, as the porch of the temple was, be inlaid with love, as gold.

Second. It had the pillars adjoined to it, the which, besides their stateliness, seem to be there typically to example. For there was seen, by the space of four cubits, their lily-work in the porch.[3] Of their lily-work I spake before. Now that they were so placed that they might be seen in the porch of the house, it seems to be for example, to teach the church, that she should live without worldly care, as did the apostles, the first planters of the church. And let ministers do this; they are now the pillars of the churches, and they stand before the porch of the house; let them also show their lily-work to the house, that the church may learn of them to be without carefulness as to worldly things, and also to be rich in love and charity towards the brethren. A covetous minister is a base thing, a pillar more symbolizing Lot's wife than an holy apostle of Jesus Christ; let them, since they stand at the door, and since the eyes of all in the porch are upon them, be patterns and examples of good works.[4]

Third. Another ornament unto this porch was, that it was an inlet into the temple. Charity is it which receiveth orphans, that receiveth the poor and afflicted into the church. Worldly love, or that which is carnal, shuts up bowels, yea, and the church-doors too, against the poor of the flock; wherefore look that this kind of love be never countenanced by you. Crave that rather which is a fruit of the Spirit. O churches, let your ministers be beautified with your love, that they may beautify you with their love; and also be an ornament unto you, and to that Gospel they minister to you, for Jesus Christ's sake.

XXII. OF THE ASCENT BY WHICH THEY WENT UP INTO THE PORCH OF THE TEMPLE.

1. This porch also had certain steps, by which they went up

---

[1] 1 Timothy 6:17–19.
[2] Luke 12:33–34.
[3] 1 Kings 7:19.
[4] 1 Timothy 6:10–12; Titus 2:7.

into the house of the Lord. I know not directly the number of them; though Ezekiel speaks something about it.[1] Hence, when men went to worship in the temple, they were said to go UP into the house of the Lord.[2]

These steps, which were the ascent to the temple, were so curiously set, and also so finely wrought, that they were amaz-ing to behold. Wherefore, when the queen of Sheba, who came to prove Solomon's wisdom, saw 'the house which he had built, . . . and his ascent by which he went up into the house of the Lord, she had no more spirit in her.' She was by that sight quite drowned, and overcome.[3]

2. These steps, whether cedar, gold, or stone, yet that which added to their adornment was the wonderment of a queen. And whatever they were made of, to be sure they were a shadow of those steps which we should take to and in the house of God. Steps of God.[4] Steps ordered by him.[5] Steps ordered in his word.[6] Steps of faith.[7] Steps of the Spirit.[8] Steps of truth.[9] Steps washed with butter.[10] Steps taken before, or in the presence of, God. Steps butted and bounded by a divine rule. These are steps indeed.

3. There are therefore no such steps as these to be found any where in the world. A step to honour, a step to riches, a step to worldly glory, these are everywhere; but what are these to the steps by which men do ascend or go up to the house of the Lord!

He then that entereth into the house of the Lord is an ascend-ing man; as it is said of Moses, he went up into the mount of God. It is ascending to go into the house of God. The world believe not this; they think it is going downward to go up to the house of God; but they are in a horrible mistake.

The steps then by which men went up into the temple are, and ought to be, opposed to those which men take to their lusts

---

[1] Ezekiel 40:38–39.
[2] Isaiah 38:22.
[3] 1 Kings 10:4–5.
[4] Psalm 85:13.
[5] Psalm 37:23.
[6] Psalm 119:133.
[7] Romans 4:12.
[8] 2 Corinthians 12:18.
[9] 3 John 4.
[10] Job 29:6.

and empty glories. Hence such steps are said not only to decline from God, but to take hold of the path to death and hell.[1]

The steps, then, by which men went up to the house of the Lord, were significative of those steps which men take when they go to God, to heaven, and glory: for these steps were the way to God, to God in his holy temple.

But how few are there that, as the queen of the south, are taken with these goodly steps! Do not most rather seek to push away our feet from taking hold of the path of life, or else lay snares for us in the way? But all these notwithstanding, the Lord guide us in the way of his steps: they are goodly steps, they are the best.

XXIII. OF THE GATE OF THE PORCH OF THE TEMPLE.

1. The porch, at which was an ascent to the temple, had a gate belonging to it. This gate, according to the prophet Ezekiel, was six cubits wide. The leaves of this gate were double, one folding this way, the other folding that.[2]

Now here some may object, and say, Since the way to God by these doors were so wide, why doth Christ say the way and gate is narrow?

Answer. The straitness, the narrowness, must not be understood of the gate simply, but because of that cumber that some men carry with them, that pretend to be going to heaven. Six cubits! What is sixteen cubits to him who would enter in here with all the world on his back? The young man in the gospel, who made such a noise for heaven, might have gone in easy enough; for in six cubits breadth there is room: but, poor man, he was not for going in thither, unless he might carry in his houses upon his shoulder too, and now the gate was strait.[3] Wherefore he that will enter in at the gate of heaven, of which this gate into the temple was a type, must go in by himself, and not with his bundles of trash on his back;[4] and if he will go in thus, he need not fear there is room. 'The

---

[1] Psalm 44:18; Proverbs 2:18; 5:5; 7:25–27.

[2] Ezekiel 40:48.

[3] Mark 10:17–27.

[4] Wealth and honours, when sanctified, are valuable aids to Christian usefulness; but unutterable woes will fall upon him who attempts to enter heaven with temporal or ecclesiastical pomps vain-gloriously carried upon his shoulders.—(OFFOR.)

righteous nation that keepeth the truth, they shall enter in.'[1]

2. They that enter in at the gate of the inner court must be clothed in fine linen: how then shall they go into the temple that carry the clogs of the dirt of this world at their heels? 'Thus saith the Lord God; No stranger uncircumcised in heart, nor uncircumcised in flesh, shall enter into my sanctuary.'[2]

3. The wideness therefore of this gate is for this cause here made mention of, to wit, to encourage them that would gladly enter thereat, according to the mind of God, and not to flatter them that are not for leaving of all for God.

4. Wherefore let such as would go in remember that here is room, even a gate to enter in at six cubits wide. We have been all this while but on the outside of the temple, even in the courts of the house of the Lord, to see the beauty and glory that is there. The beauty hereof made men cry out, and say, 'How amiable *are* thy tabernacles, O Lord of hosts! my soul longeth, yea, even fainteth for the courts of the Lord;' and to say, 'a day in thy courts *is* better than a thousand.'[3]

XXIV. OF THE PINNACLES OF THE TEMPLE.

1. There were also several pinnacles belonging to the temple. These pinnacles stood on the top aloft in the air, and were sharp, and so difficult to stand upon: what men say of their number and length I wave, and come directly to their signification.

2. I therefore take those pinnacles to be types of those lofty airy notions with which some men delight themselves, while they hover, like birds, above the solid and godly truths of Christ. Satan attempted to entertain Christ Jesus with this type, and antitype, at once, when he set him on one of the pinnacles of the temple, and offered to thrust him upon a false confidence in God, by a false and unsound interpretation of a text.[4]

3. You have some men cannot be content to worship IN the temple, but must be aloft; no place will serve them but pinnacles, pinnacles; that they may be speaking in and to the air, that they may be promoting their heady notions, instead of solid truth; not considering that now they are where the devil would

---

[1] Isaiah 26:2.

[2] Ezekiel 44:9.

[3] Psalm 84:1–2, etc.

[4] Matthew 4:5–6; Luke 4:9–11.

have them be; they strut upon their points, their pinnacles; but let them look to it, there is difficulty standing upon pinnacles; their neck, their soul, is in danger. We read, God is *in* his temple, not *upon* these pinnacles.[1]

4. It is true, Christ was once upon one of these; but the devil set him there, with intent to have dashed him in pieces by a fall; and yet even then told him, if he would venture to tumble down, he should be kept from dashing his foot against a stone. To be there, therefore, was one of Christ's temptations; consequently one of Satan's stratagems; nor went he thither of his own accord, for he knew that there was danger; he loved not to clamber pinnacles.

5. This should teach Christians to be low and little in their own eyes, and to forbear to intrude into airy and vain speculations, and to take heed of being puffed up with a foul and empty mind.[2]

XXV. OF THE PORTERS OF THE TEMPLE.

1. There were porters belonging to the temple. In David's time their number was four thousand men.[3]

2. The porters were of the Levites, and their work was to watch at every gate of the house of the Lord; at the gate of the outer court, at the gates of the inner court, and at the door of the temple of the Lord.[4]

3. The work of the porters, or rather the reason of their watching, was to look that none not duly qualified entered into the house of the Lord. 'He set,' saith the text, 'the porters at the gates of the house of the Lord, that none *which was* unclean in any thing should enter in.'[5]

4. The excellency of the porters lay in these three things, their watchfulness, diligence, and valour, to make resistance to those that, as unfit, would attempt to enter those courts and the house of God.[6]

---

[1] Psalm 11:4; Habakkuk 2:20.

[2] Every Christian pilgrim, if he journeys aright, must be entirely guided by prayerful personal inquiries at the holy oracles as to his way to heaven. How do sin and Satan strive to mislead him in this essential duty.—(OFFOR.)

[3] 1 Chronicles 23:5.

[4] 2 Chronicles 35:15.

[5] 2 Chronicles 23:19.

[6] 1 Chronicles 26:6; Mark 13:34.

5. These porters were types of our gospel ministers, as they are set to be watchmen in and over the church, and the holy things of God. Therefore as Christ gives to every man in the church his work, so he commands 'the porter to watch.'[1]

6. Sometimes every awakened Christian is said to be a porter, and such at Christ's first knock open unto him immediately.[2]

7. The heart of a Christian is also sometimes called the porter; for that when the true shepherd comes to it, to him this porter openeth also.[3]

8. This last has the body for his watch-house; the eyes and ears for his port-holes; the tongue therewith to cry, Who comes there? as also to call for aid, when anything unclean shall attempt with force and violence to enter in, to defile the house.

XXVI. OF THE CHARGE OF THE PORTERS OF THE TEMPLE MORE PARTICULARLY.

1. The charge of the porters was, to keep their watch, in four square, even round about the temple of God. Thus it was ordained by David, before him by Moses, and after him by Solomon his son.[4]

2. The porters had some of them the charge of the treasure-chambers; some of them had the charge of the ministering vessels, even to bring them in and out by tale; also the opening and shutting of the gates of the house of the Lord was a part of their calling and office.

3. I told you, the porters were types of our gospel ministers, as they are watchmen in and over the house of God; and therefore in that they were thus to watch round about the temple, what is it but to show how diligent Satan is, to see if he may get in somewhere, by some means, to defile the church of God; he goes round and round and round us, to see if he can find a hog-hole for that purpose.

4. This also showeth that the church of itself, without its watchmen, is a weak, feeble, and very helpless thing. What can the lady or mistress do to defend herself against thieves and sturdy villains, if there be none but she at home? It is said,

---

[1] Isaiah 21:11; Ezekiel 3:17; 33:7; Acts 20:27–31; 2 Timothy 4:5; Revelation 2:2–3.

[2] Luke 12:35–40.

[3] John 10:3.

[4] 1 Chronicles 9:24; Numbers 3; 2 Chronicles 23:19; 35:15.

when the shepherd is smitten, the sheep shall be scattered. What could the temple do without its watchmen?

5. Again, in that the porters had charge of the treasure-chambers as it is,[1] it is to intimate, that the treasures of the gospel are with the ministers of our God, and that the church, next to Christ, should seek them at their mouth. 'We have this treasure in earthen vessels,' saith Paul, and they are 'stewards of the' manifold 'mysteries of God.'[2]

6. These are God's true scribes, and bring out of their treasury things new and old; or, as he saith in another place, 'At our gates,' that is, where our porters watch, '*are* all manner of pleasant *fruits, which* I have laid up for thee, O my beloved.'[3]

7. Further, some of them had charge of the ministering vessels, and they were to bring them in and out by tale.[4] (1.) If by ministering vessels you understand gospel ordinances, then you see who has the charge of them, to wit, the watchmen and ministers of the word.[5] (2.) If by ministering vessels you mean the members of the church, for they are also ministering vessels, then you see who has the care of them, to wit, the pastors, the gospel ministers. Therefore 'obey them that have the rule over you . . . for they watch for your souls, as they that must give account; that they may do it with joy, and not with grief, for that *is* unprofitable for you.'[6]

8. The opening of the gates did also belong to the porters, to show that the power of the keys, to wit, of opening and shutting, of letting in and keeping out of the church, doth ministerially belong to these watchmen.[7]

9. The conclusion is, then let the churches love their pastors, hear their pastors, be ruled by their pastors, and suffer themselves to be watched over, and to be exhorted, counselled, and if need be, reproved, and rebuked by their pastors.[8] And let the ministers not

---

[1] 1 Chronicles 9:26.

[2] 1 Corinthians 4:1; 2 Corinthians 4:7; 1 Peter 4:10; Ephesians 4:11–13.

[3] Song of Solomon 7:13; Matthew 13:52.

[4] 1 Chronicles 9:28.

[5] Luke 1:12; 2 Thessalonians 2:15; 2 Timothy 2:2.

[6] Hebrews 13:17.

[7] Matthew 16:19; Hebrews 12:15.

[8] The simple-minded nature of Bunyan here appears conspicuously. He measures others by his own bushel, as if every pastor had as single an eye to the welfare of their flocks as he had over the

Footnotes are continued on the next page.

sleep, but be watchful, and look to the ordinances, to the souls of the saints, and the gates of the churches. Watchman, watchman, watch!

XXVII. OF THE DOORS OF THE TEMPLE.

NOW we are come to the gate of the temple; namely, to that which let out of the porch into the holy place.

1. These doors or gates were folding, and they opened by degrees. First, a quarter, and then a half, after that three quarters, and last of all the whole. These doors also hanged upon hinges of gold, and upon posts made of the goodly olive-tree.[1]

2. These doors did represent Christ, as he is the way to the Father, as also did the door of the tabernacle, at which the people were wont to stand when they went to inquire of God. Wherefore, Christ saith, 'I am the door,' alluding to this, 'by me if any man enter he shall be saved, and shall go in and out, and find pasture.'[2] (1.) 'I am the door.' The door into the court, the door into the porch, the door into the temple, the door into the holiest, the door to the Father. But now we are at the door of the temple. (2.) And observe it, this door by Solomon was not measured as the door of the porch was: for though the door into the court, and the door into the porch were measured, to show that the right to ordinances and the inlet into the church is to be according to a prescript rule, yet this door was not measured; to show that Christ, as he is the inlet to saving grace, is beyond all measure, and unsearchable. Hence his grace is called 'unsearchable riches,' and that above all we can ask or think, for that it passeth knowledge.[3]

3. It is, therefore, convenient that we put a note upon this, that we may distinguish rule and duty from grace and pardoning mercy; for as I said, though Christ, as the door to outward privileges, is set forth by rule and measure; yet, as he is the door

---

Footnotes are continued from the last page.

Church at Bedford. How tenderly ought the churches of Christ to cherish such pastors as Bunyan, while they prayerfully watch over their ministrations.—(OFFOR.)

[1] 1 Kings 6:33–34; Ezekiel 41:23–24.

[2] Exodus 33:9–10; 38:8; 40:12; Leviticus 1:3–4; 8:3–4, 33; 15:14; Numbers 6:13, 18; 10:3; 25:6; 27:2; 1 Samuel 2:22; John 10:9.

[3] Ephesians 3:8, 19–20.

to grace and favour, never creature, as yet, did see the length and breadth of him.[1,2]

4. Therefore, I say, this gate was not measured; for what should a rule do here, where things are beyond all measure?

5. This gate being also to open by degrees, is of signification to us; for it will be opening first by one fold, then by another, and yet will never be set wide, wide open, until the day of judgment. For then, and not till then, will the whole of the matter be open. 'For now we see through a glass, darkly; but then face to face: now I know in part, but then shall I know even as also I am known.'[3]

XXVIII. OF THE LEAVES OF THIS GATE OF THE TEMPLE.

THE leaves of this gate or door, as I told you before, were folding, and so, as was hinted, has something of signification in them. For by this means a man, especially a young disciple, may easily be mistaken; thinking that the whole passage, when yet but a part was open; whereas, three parts might be yet kept undiscovered to him. For these doors, as I said before, were never yet set wide open; I mean, in the anti-type; never man yet saw all the riches and fulness which is in Christ. So that I say, a new comer, if he judged by present sight, especially if he saw but little, might easily be mistaken; wherefore such, for the most part, are most horribly afraid that they shall never get in thereat. How sayest thou, young comer, is not this the case with thy soul? So it seems to thee that thou art too big, being so great, so tun-bellied a sinner. But, O thou sinner, fear not, the doors are folding-doors, and may be opened wider, and wider again after that; wherefore, when thou comest to this gate, and imaginest there is not space enough for thee to enter, knock, and it shall be wider opened unto thee, and thou shalt be received.[4] So, then, whoever thou art that art come to the door, of which the temple door was a type, trust not to thy first conceptions of things, but believe there is grace abundant. Thou knowest not

---

[1] Ephesians 3:17, 19.

[2] This is one of those beautiful gems which sparkle all through Bunyan's works, 'As the depth of the riches both of the wisdom and knowledge of God!'—(OFFOR.)

[3] 1 Corinthians 13:12.

[4] Luke 11:9; John 6:37.

yet what Christ can do, the doors are folding-doors. He can 'do exceeding abundantly above all that we can ask or think.'[1]

The hinges on which these doors do hang were, as I told you, gold; to signify that they both turned upon motives and motions of love, and also that the openings thereof were rich. Golden hinges the gate to God doth turn upon.

The posts on which these doors did hang were of the olive-tree, that fat and oily tree, to show that they do never open with lothness or sluggishness, as doors do whose hinges want oil. They are always oily, and so open easily and quickly to those who knock at them. Hence you read, that he that dwells in this house gives freely, loves freely, and doth us good with all his heart. 'Yea,' saith he, 'I will rejoice over them to do them good, and I will plant them in this land assuredly with my whole heart, and with my whole soul.'[2] Wherefore, the oil of grace, signified by this oily tree, or these olive-posts, on which these doors do hang, do cause that they open glibly or frankly to the soul.

XXIX. WHAT THE DOORS OF THE TEMPLE WERE MADE OF.

1. The doors of the temple were made of fir; that is so sweet scented, and pleasant to the smell.[3]

2. Mankind is also often compared to the fir-tree.[4]

3. Now, since the doors of the temple were made of the same, doth it not show that the way into God's house, and into his favour, is by the same nature which they are of that thither enter, even through the veil, his flesh?[5] For this door, I mean the anti-type, doth even say of himself, '*I am* like a green fir-tree, from me is thy fruit found.'[6]

4. This fir-tree is Christ; Christ as man, and so as the way to the Father. The doors of the temple are also, as you see here, made of the fir-tree; even of that tree which was a type of the humanity of Jesus Christ. Consider Hebrews 2:14.

5. The fir-tree is also the house of the stork, that unclean bird,

[1] Ephesians 3:20.

[2] Jeremiah 3:12, 14, 22; 32:41; Revelation 21:6; 22:17.

[3] 1 Kings 6:34.

[4] Isaiah 41:19; 55:13; 60:13–17; 14:8.

[5] Hebrews 10:20.

[6] Hosea 14:8.

even as Christ is a harbour and shelter for sinners. As for the stork, saith the text, the fir-tree is her house; and Christ saith to the sinners that see their want of shelter, 'Come unto me, and I will give you rest.' He is a refuge for the oppressed, a refuge in time of trouble.[1] He is, as the doors of fir of the temple, the inlet to God's house, to God's presence, and to a partaking of his glory. Thus God did of old, by similitudes, teach his people his way.

XXX. HOW THE DOORS OF THE TEMPLE WERE ADORNED.

AND Solomon carved upon the doors 'cherubims, and palm trees, and open flowers, and covered them with gold.'[2]

First. He carved cherubims thereon. These cherubims were figures or types of angels, and forasmuch as they were carved here upon the door, it was to show,

1. What delight the angels take in waiting upon the Lord, and in going at his bidding, at his beck. They are always waiting like servants at the door of their Lord's house.

2. It may be also to show how much pleased they are to be where they may see sinners come to God. For 'there is joy in the presence of the angels of God over one sinner that repenteth,' and comes to God by Christ for mercy.[3]

3. They may be also placed here to behold with what reverence or irreverence those that come hither to worship do behave themselves. Hence Solomon cautions those that come to God's house to worship, that they take heed to their feet, because of the angels. Paul also says, Women must take heed that they behave themselves in the church as they should, and that because of the angels.[4]

4. They may also be carved upon the temple doors, to show us how ready they are, so soon as any poor creature comes to Christ for life to take the care and charge of its conduct through this miserable world. 'Are they not all ministering spirits, sent forth to minister for them who shall be heirs of salvation?'[5]

5. They may also be carved here, to show that they are ready,

---

[1] Deuteronomy 14:18; Leviticus 11:19; Psalm 104:17; 84:2–3
   Matthew 11:27–28; Hebrews 6:17–20.
[2] 1 Kings 6:35; Ezekiel 41:25.
[3] Luke 15:10.
[4] Ecclesiastes 5:1–2, 6; 1 Corinthians 11:5–6, 10.
[5] Hebrews 1:14.

at Christ's command, to take vengeance for him upon those that despise his people and hate his person. Hence he bids the world take heed what they do to his 'little ones,' for 'their angels do always behold the face of their Father which is in heaven,' and are ready at the door to run at his bidding.[1]

6. Or lastly, they may be carved upon these doors, to show that Christ Jesus is the very supporter and upholder of angels, as well as the Saviour of sinful man. For as he is before all things, so by him all things consist; angels stand by Christ, men are saved by Christ, and therefore the very cherubims themselves were carved upon these doors, to show they are upheld and subsist by him.[2]

Second. Again, as the cherubims are carved here, so there were palm trees carved here also. The palm tree is upright, it twisteth not itself awry.[3]

1. Apply this to Christ, and then it shows us the uprightness of his heart, word, and ways with sinners. 'Good and upright *is* the Lord, therefore will he teach sinners in the way;' in at the door to life.[4]

2. The palm or palm tree is also a token of victory; and as placed here, it betokeneth the conquest that Christ, the door, should get over sin, death, the devil, and hell for us.[5]

3. If we apply the palm tree to the church, as we may, for she also is compared thereto,[6] then the palm tree may be carved here to show, that none but such as are upright of heart and life shall dwell in the presence of God. 'The hypocrite,' says Job, 'shall not come before him.' 'The upright,' says David, 'shall not dwell in thy presence.'[7] They are they that are clothed in white robes, which signifies uprightness of life, that stand before the Lamb with 'palms in their hands.'[8]

Third. There were also carved upon these doors open flowers; and that to teach us that here is the sweet scent and fragrant smell; and that the coming soul will find it so in Christ, this door. 'I

---

[1] Matthew 18:10.
[2] 1 Corinthians 8:6; Colossians 1:17; Hebrews 1:3.
[3] Jeremiah 10:5.
[4] Psalm 25:8; 92:15.
[5] Romans 7:24; 8:37; 1 Corinthians 15:54–57; Revelation 7:9–11.
[6] Song of Solomon 7:8–10.
[7] Job 13:16; Psalm 140:13.
[8] Revelation 7:9.

AM,' saith he, 'the rose of Sharon, *and* the lily of the valleys.' And
again, 'His cheeks *are* as a bed of spices, *as* sweet flowers: his lips
like lilies, dropping sweet-smelling myrrh.'[1] Open flowers. Open
flowers are the sweetest, because full grown, and because, as such,
they yield their fragrancy most freely. Wherefore, when he saith
upon the doors are open flowers, he setteth Christ Jesus forth in
his good savours, as high as by such similitudes he could; and that
both in name and office. For open flowers lay, by their thus opening themselves before us, all their beauty also most plainly before
our faces. There are varieties of beauty in open flowers, the which
they also commend to all observers. Now, upon these doors, you
see, are open flowers, flowers ripe, and spread before us, to show
that his name and offices are savoury to them that by him do enter
his house to God his Father.[2]

'All these were overlaid with fine gold.' Gold is the most rich
of all metals; and here it is said the doors, the cherubims, the
palm trees, and open flowers, were overlaid therewith. And this
shows, that as these things are rich in themselves, even so they
should be to us. We have a golden door to go to God by, and
golden angels to conduct us through the world: we have golden
palm trees as tokens of our victory, and golden flowers to smell
on all the way to heaven.

XXXI. OF THE WALL OF THE TEMPLE.

THE wall of the temple was 'ceiled with fir tree, which he overlaid
with fine gold, and set thereon palm trees and chains.'[3]

The walls were as the body of the house, unto which Christ
alluded when he said, 'Destroy this temple, and in three days I
will raise it up.'[4] Hence to be, and worship in the temple, was a
type of being in Christ, and worshipping God by him. For Christ,
as was said, is the great temple of God, in the which all the elect
meet, and in whom they do service to and for his Father.

Hence again the true worshippers are said to be in him, to
speak in him, to walk in him, to obey in him.[5] For, as of old, all

---

[1] Song of Solomon 2:1; 5:13.
[2] Song of Solomon 1:1–4.
[3] 2 Chronicles 3:5–7.
[4] John 2:19.
[5] 2 Corinthians 2:14; 12:19; Colossians 2:6.

true worship was to be found at the temple, so now it is only found with Christ, and with them that are in him. The promise of old was made to them that worshipped within these walls. 'Unto them,' saith he, 'will I give in my house, and within my walls,' to them that worship there in truth, 'a place, and a name, better than of sons and of daughters.'[1]

But now, in New Testament times, 'all the promises of God in him *are* yea, and in him, amen unto the glory of God by us.'[2] This is yet further hinted to us in that it is said these walls are ceiled with fir;[3] which, as was showed before, was a figure of the humanity of Jesus Christ.

A wall is for defence, and so is the humanity of Jesus Christ. It is, was, and will be, our defence for ever. For it was that which underwent and overcame the curse of the law, and that in which our everlasting righteousness is found. Had he not in that interposed, we had perished for ever. Hence we are said to be reconciled to God in the body of his flesh through death.[4]

Now, this wall was overlaid with fine gold. Gold here is a figure of the righteousness of Christ, by which we are justified in the sight of God. Therefore you read, that his church, as justified, is said to stand at his right hand in cloth of gold. 'Upon thy right hand did stand the queen in gold of Ophir.' And again, 'Her clothing *is* of wrought gold.'[5] This the wall was overlaid with; this the body of Christ was filled with. Men, while in the temple, were clothed with gold, even with the gold of the temple; and men in Christ are clothed with righteousness, the righteousness of Christ. Wherefore this consideration doth yet more illustrate the matter. In that the palm trees were set on this wall, it may be to show that the elect are fixed in Jesus, and so shall abide for ever.

Chains were also carved on these walls, yea, and they were golden chains; there were chains on the pillars, and now also we find chains upon the walls.[6] 1. Chains were used to hold one captive, and such Paul did wear at Rome, but he called them 'his

---

[1] Isaiah 56:5.

[2] 2 Corinthians 1:20.

[3] Ceiled is now only used with reference to the top of a room—the ceiling. It is an old English word, and means overlaid or lined with wood, wainscot, or plank, either roof, sides, or floor.—(OFFOR.)

[4] Colossians 1:19–20; Romans 5:8–10.

[5] Psalm 45:9, 13.

[6] Philippians 1:12–13.

bands in Christ.' 2. Chains sometimes signify great afflictions, which God lays on us for our sins.[1] 3. Chains also may be more mystically understood, as of those obligations which the love of God lays upon us, to do and suffer for him.[2] 4. Chains do sometimes signify beauty and comely ornaments. 'Thy neck,' saith Christ to his spouse, 'is comely with chains *of gold.*' And again, 'I put brace-lets upon thy hands, and a chain on thy neck.'[3] 5. Chains also do sometimes denote greatness and honour, such as Daniel had when the king made him the third ruler in the kingdom.[4]

Now all these are temple-chains, and are put upon us for good; some to prevent our ruin, some to dispose our minds the better, and some to dignify and to make us noble. Temple-chains are brave chains. None but temple-worshippers must wear temple-chains.

XXXII. OF THE GARNISHING OF THE TEMPLE WITH PRECIOUS STONES.

'AND he garnished the house with precious stones for beauty.'[5] 1. This is another ornament to the temple of the Lord; where-fore, as he saith, it was garnished with them; he saith it was garnished with them for beauty. The line[6] saith, garnished; the margin saith, covered. 2. Wherefore, I think, they were fixed as stars, or as the stars in the firmament, so they were set in the ceiling of the house, as in the heaven of the holy temple. 3. And thus fixed, they do the more aptly tell us of what they were a figure; namely, of the ministerial gifts and officers in the church. For ministers, as to their gifts and office, are called stars of God, and are said to be in the hand of Christ.[7] 4. Wherefore, as the stars glitter and twinkle in the firmament of heaven, so do true ministers in the firmament of his church.[8] 5. So that it is said

---

[1] Psalm 107:9–11; Lamentations 1:14; 3:7.

[2] Acts 20:22.

[3] Song of Solomon 1:10; Ezekiel 16:8–11; Proverbs 1:9.

[4] Daniel 5:7, 16, 29.

[5] 2 Chronicles 3:6–7.

[6] The line means the text. The marginal reading agrees with the puritan version 'overlayed.' Tyndale renders it, 'And he paved the house with precious stones goodly.' Coverdale, 'And overlayed the house with precious stones to beautify it.'—(OFFOR.)

[7] Revelation 1:20.

[8] 1 Chronicles 29:2; John 5:35; Daniel 12:3.

again these gifts come down from above, as signifying they distil their dew from above. And hence, again, the ministers are said to be set over us in the Lord, as placed in the firmament of his heaven to give a light upon his earth. 'There is gold and a multitude of rubies, but the lips of knowledge *are* a precious jewel.'[1]

Verily, it is enough to make a man in this house look always upward; since the ceiling above head doth thus glitter with precious stones. Precious stones, all manner of precious stones, stones of all colours. For there are divers gifts, differences of administrations, and diversities of operations, 'but it is the same God which worketh all in all.'[2] Thus had the ceiling of this house a pearl here, and there a diamond; here a jasper, and there a sapphire; here a sardius, and there a jacinth; here a sardonyx, and there an amethyst. 'For to one is given by the Spirit the word of wisdom, to another the word of knowledge;' to one the gift of healing, to another faith; to this man to work miracles, to that a spirit of prophecy; to another the discerning of spirits, to another divers kinds of tongues.[3]

He also overlaid the house, beams, posts, walls, doors, etc., and all with gold. O what a beautiful house the temple was; how full of glory was it! And yet all was but a shadow, a shadow of things to come, and which was to be answered in the church of the living God, the pillar and ground of truth, by better things than these.

XXXIII. OF THE WINDOWS OF THE TEMPLE.

'AND for the house, he made windows of narrow lights.'[4] There were windows of this house, windows for the chambers and windows round about.[5] These windows were of several sizes, but all narrow, narrow without, but wide within; they also were finely wrought, and beautified with goodly stones.[6]

1. Windows, as they are to a house an ornament, so also to it they are a benefit. 'Truly the light *is* sweet, and a pleasant *thing it is* for the eyes to behold the sun.'[7] The window is that which Christ

---

[1] Proverbs 20:15.
[2] 1 Corinthians 12:4–6.
[3] 1 Corinthians 12:8–11.
[4] 1 Kings 6:4.
[5] Ezekiel 40:16, 22–25, 29, 33, 36.
[6] Isaiah 54:12.
[7] Ecclesiastes 11:7.

looks forth at, the window is that which the sun looks in at.[1]

2. By the light which shines in at the window we also see to make and keep the house clean, and also to do what business is necessary there to be done. 'In thy light shall we see light;' light to do our duty, and that both to God and man.

3. These windows therefore were figures of the written word, by and through, which Christ shows himself to his, and by which we also apprehend him. And hence the Word of God is compared to a glass through which the light doth come, and by which we see not only the beams of the sun, but our own smutches also.[2]

4. The lights indeed were narrow, wherefore we see also through their antitype but darkly and imperfectly. 'Now we see through a glass darkly,' or, as in a riddle,[3] now we know but in part.[4]

5. Their windows and their light are but of little service to those that are without; the world sees but little of the beauty of the church by the light of the written Word, though the church, by that light, can see the dismal state of the world, and also how to avoid it.

XXXIV. OF THE CHAMBERS OF THE TEMPLE.

In the temple Solomon made chambers.[5]

1. The chambers were of several sizes; some little, some large; some higher, some lower; some more inward, and some outward.

2. These chambers were for several services; some were for rests, some to hide in, some to lay up treasure in, and some for solace and delight.[6] They were for resting-places. Here the priests and porters were wont to lodge. They were for hiding-places. Here Jehoshabeath hid Joash from Athaliah the term of six years.[7] They were also to lay the temple treasure, or dedicated things in, that they might be safely kept there for the worshippers.[8] And some of them were for solace and delight; and, I must add, some for durable habitation. Wherefore in some of them some dwelt

---

[1] Song of Solomon 2:9.

[2] 2 Chronicles 30:18; James 1:23–25.

[3] See margin of 1 Corinthians 13:12, Gr., 'in a riddle.'—(OFFOR.)

[4] 1 Corinthians 13:12.

[5] 1 Kings 6:5.

[6] 2 Chronicles 3:9; Ezekiel 40:7; 41:5, 9–11; 2 Chronicles 31:11–12.

[7] 2 Kings 11:3.

[8] Ezra 8:29.

always, yea, their names dwelt there when they were dead.

(1.) Those of them which were for rest, were types of that rest which by faith we have in the Son of God, and of that eternal rest which we shall have in heaven by him.[1] (2.) Those chambers which were for hiding and security, were types of that safety which we have in Christ from the rage of the world.[2] (3.) Those chambers which were for the reception of the treasures and dedicated things were types of Christ, as he is the common store-house of believers. 'For it pleased *the Father*, that in him should all fulness dwell;' 'and of his fulness we all receive, and grace for grace.'[3] (4.) Those chambers that were for solace and delight, were types of those retirements and secret meetings of Christ with the soul, where he gives it his embraces, and delights her with his bosom and ravishing delights. 'He brought me,' said she, 'into his chambers,' 'into the chamber of her that conceived me,' and there he gave her his love.[4]

The chambers which were for durable dwelling-places were types of those eternal dwelling-places which are in the heavens, prepared of Christ and the Father, for them that shall be saved.[5] This it is to 'dwell on high,' and to be safe from fear of evil! Here therefore you see are chambers for rest, chambers for safety, chambers for treasure, chambers for solace, and chambers for durable habitations. O the rest and peace that the chambers of God's high house will yield to its inhabitants in another world! Here they will 'rest from their labours,' 'rest in their beds,' rest with God, rest from sin, temptation, and all sorrow.[6] God therefore then shall wipe all tears from our eyes, even when he comes out of his chamber as a bridegroom, to fetch his bride, his wife unto him thither, to the end they may have eternal solace together. O these are far better than the chambers of the south!

XXXV. OF THE STAIRS BY WHICH THEY WENT UP INTO THE CHAMBERS OF THE TEMPLE.

THERE were stairs by which men went up into these chambers of

---

[1] Matthew 11:28; Hebrews 4:3.
[2] Isaiah 26:20.
[3] John 1:16; Colossians 1:19.
[4] Song of Solomon 1:4; 3:4.
[5] John 14:1–4; 2 Corinthians 5:1–4.
[6] Revelation 14:13; Isaiah 57:1–2; 2 Thessalonians 1:7.

the temple, and they were but one pair, and they went from below to the first, and so to the middle, and thence to the highest chambers in the temple.[1]

1. These stairs were winding; so that they turned about, that did go up them. So then, he that assayed to go into these chambers, must turn with the stairs, or he could not go up, no, not into the lowest chambers.

2. These stairs therefore were a type of a twofold repentance. That by which we turn from nature to grace, and that by which we turn from the imperfections which attend a state of grace to glory. Hence true repentance, or the right going up these turning stairs, is called repentance to salvation; for true repentance stoppeth not at the reception of grace; for that is but a going up these stairs to the middle chambers.[2]

Thus, therefore, the soul, at its going up these stairs, turns and turns, till it enters the doors of the highest chambers. It groans, though in a state of grace, because that is not the state of glory. I count then, that from the first to the middle chambers may be a type of turning from nature to grace. But from the middle to the highest, these stairs may signify a turning still from the imperfections and temptations that attend a state of grace, to that of immortality and glory.[3]

For as there are turning stairs, from the lowest to the middle chambers, so the stairs from thence still turn, and so will do, till you come to the highest chambers. I do not say that they that have received grace, do repent they received grace; but say they that have received grace, are yet sorry that grace is not consummate in glory; and hence they are for going up thither still, by these turning stairs; yea, they cannot rest below, as they would, till they ascend to the highest chambers. 'O wretched man that I am!' And 'in this we groan earnestly,' is the language of gracious souls.[4] True, every one doth not do thus that comes into the temple of God; many rest below stairs, they like not to go turning upward. Nor do I believe that all that bid fair for ascending to the middle chambers, get up to the highest stories, to his stories in the heavens. Many in churches, who seem to be turned from nature to grace, have not the grace to go up, turning still; but rest in that

---

[1] 1 Kings 6:8; Ezekiel 41:7.

[2] 2 Corinthians 7:10.

[3] 2 Corinthians 5:1–9.

[4] Romans 7:24; 2 Corinthians 5:1-3.

show of things, and so die below a share in the highest chambers.

All these things are true in the anti-type, and, as I think, pre-figured by these turning stairs to the chambers of the temple. But this turning, and turning still, displeases some much; they say it makes them giddy; but I say, there is no way like this, to make a man stand steady; stedfast in the faith, and with boldness in the day of judgment. For he has this seated in his heart; I went up by the turning stairs, till I came to the highest chambers. A strait pair of stairs are like that ladder by which men ascend to the gallows; they are the turning ones that lead us to the heavenly mansion-houses. Look, therefore, you that come into the temple of God to worship, that you stay not at the foot of these turning stairs, but go up thence; yea, up them, and up them, and up them, till you come to the view of the heavens; yea, till you are possessed of the highest chambers! How many times has God, by the Scripture, called upon you to TURN, and told you, you must turn or die! and now here he has added to his call a figure, by placing a pair of turning stairs in his temple, to convict your very senses, that you must TURN, if you mean to go up into his holy chambers, and so into his eternal mansion-houses; and look that you turn to purpose; for every turning will not serve. Some turn, but not to the Most High; and so turn to no purpose.

XXXVI. OF THE MOLTEN SEA THAT WAS IN THE TEMPLE.

THERE was also a molten sea in the temple; it was made of brass, and contained three thousand baths.[1,2] This sea was for the priests to wash in when they came into the temple to accomplish the service of God; to wash their hands and feet at, that they might not, when they came thither, die for their unpreparedness. The laver also which was in the wilderness was of the same use there.[3]

1. It was, as may be supposed, called a sea, for that it was large to contain; and a sea of brass, for that it was made thereof. It is called in Revelations a sea of glass, alluding to that in the wilderness, which was made of the brazen looking-glasses of women that came to worship at the door of the tabernacle.[4]

---

[1] A bath was a Hebrew measure containing about seven gallons and a half.—(OFFOR.)

[2] 2 Chronicles 4:2–10.

[3] Exodus 30.

[4] Revelation 4:6; 15:2; Exodus 38:8.

2. It was also said to be molten, because it was made of that fashion, by fire; and its anti-type therefore is said to be a sea of glass mingled with fire.[1] (1.) This sea was a figure of the word of the gospel, in the cleansing virtue of it; which virtue then it has when mingled with the fire of the Holy Ghost. And to this Christ alludes, when he saith, 'Now ye are clean through the word which I have spoken unto you.'[2] (2.) It was a figure of the word, without mixture of men's inventions; hence it is called 'pure water.' Having your 'bodies washed with pure water.' And again, He sanctifies and cleanseth his church 'with the washing of water by the word.'[3] All these places are an allusion to the molten sea, at which of old they washed when they went into the temple to worship. Therefore, saith he, being washed, let us draw near to God.[4]

3. This sea from brim to brim was complete ten cubits; per-haps to show that there is as much in the word of the gospel to save, as there is in the ten[5] words to condemn.

4. From under this sea round about appeared oxen, ten in a cubit did compass it round about.[6] Understand by these oxen ministers, for to them they are compared in 1 Corinthians 9:8–10. And then we are taught whence true ministers come; to wit, from under the power of the gospel, for this sea breeds gospel minis-ters, as the waters breed fish.

5. It is also said in the text, that these oxen were cast when the sea was cast; insinuating that when God ordained a word of grace to save us, he also in his decree provided ministers to preach it to us to that end. Paul tells us, that he was made a minister of the gospel, 'according to God's eternal purpose which he purposed in Christ Jesus our Lord.'[7]

6. This sea is said to have a brim like the brim of a cup. To invite us as well to drink of its grace, as to wash in its water. For the word and Spirit when mixed, has not only a cleansing, but a saving quality in it.[8]

7. This brim was wrought with lilies, or was like a lily flower;

[1] Revelation 15:2.
[2] John 15:3.
[3] Ephesians 5:26; Titus 3:5.
[4] Hebrews 10:22.
[5] The moral law of ten commandments.—(OFFOR.)
[6] 2 Chronicles 4:3.
[7] Ephesians 3:9–11; Colossians 1:25.
[8] 2 Chronicles 4:1–5; 1 Corinthians 15:1–2.

to show how they should grow and flourish, and with what beautiful robes they should be adorned, who were washed, and did drink of this holy water. Yea, that God would take care of them, as he also did of lilies, and would not fail to bestow upon them what was necessary for the body, as well as for the soul.[1]

XXXVII. UPON WHAT THE MOLTEN SEA STOOD IN THE TEMPLE.

1. This molten sea stood upon the backs of twelve brazen bulls or oxen.[2]

2. These oxen, as they thus stood, looked three towards the north, three towards the west, three towards the east, and three towards the south.

3. These twelve oxen were types of the twelve apostles of the Lamb, who, as these beasts, stood looking into the four corners of the earth, and were bid to go preach the gospel in all the world.

4. They were compared to oxen, because they were clean; for the ox was a clean beast. Hence the apostles are called holy. They were compared to oxen, because the ox is strong; and they also were mighty in the word.[3]

5. The ox will not lose what he has got by drawing; he will not let the wheels go back; so the apostles were set to defend, and not let that doctrine go back, which they had preached to others; nor did they, they delivered it pure to us.

6. One of the cherubs of which you read in the vision had a face like an ox, to show that the apostles, these men of the first order, are most like the angels of God.[4]

7. In that they stood with their faces every way, it was, as I said, to show how the apostles should carry the gospel into all the world.[5]

8. And observe, just as these oxen were placed looking in the temple every way, even so stand open the gates of the New Jerusalem to receive those that by their doctrine should be brought into it. 'And they shall come from the east, and *from* the

---

[1] Matthew 6:28–34.

[2] 2 Chronicles 4:4.

[3] Proverbs 14:4; 2 Corinthians 12:12.

[4] Ezekiel 1:10.

[5] Matthew 28:19–20; Mark 16:15–18.

west, and from the north, and *from* the south, and shall sit down
in the kingdom of God.'[1]

9. These oxen bear this molten sea upon their backs, to show
that they should be the foundation workmen of the gospel, and
that it ought not to be removed, as was the molten sea of old,
from that basis to another.

10. It is also said concerning those oxen that thus did bear
this molten sea, that all their hinder parts were inwards, that
is, covered by that sea that was set upon their backs; their
hinder parts, or, as the apostle has it, 'our uncomely parts.'[2]

11. And, indeed, it becomes a gospel minister to have his uncomely parts covered with that grace which by the gospel he
preacheth unto others. As Paul exhorts Timothy to take heed
unto himself, and to his doctrine.[3]

12. But alas! there are too, too many who, can they but have
their heads covered with a few gospel notions, care not though
their hinder parts are seen of all the world. But such are false
ministers; the prophet calls them 'the tail.' 'The prophet that
speaketh lies, either by word or with his feet, he is the tail.'[4]

13. But what a shame is it to hide his head under this molten
sea, while his hinder parts hang out. Such an one is none of
Christ's oxen; for they, with honour to their Master, show their
heads before all the world, for that their hinder parts are inward, covered.

14. Look to thy hinder parts, minister, lest, while thy mouth
doth preach the gospel, thy nakedness and shame be seen of
those which hear thee. For they that do not observe to learn this
lesson themselves, will not teach others to believe the Word, nor
to live a holy life; they will learn of them to show their shame,
instead of learning to be holy.

XXXVIII. OF THE LAVERS OF THE TEMPLE.

BESIDES this molten sea, there were ten lavers in the temple; five
of which were put on the right side, and five also on the left.[5]

---

[1] Luke 13:29; Revelation 21:13–14.
[2] 1 Corinthians 13:23–24.
[3] 1 Timothy 4:6.
[4] Isaiah 9:15; Proverbs 6:12–13.
[5] 2 Chronicles 4:6.

1. Of their fashion and their furniture, you may see.[1] These lavers, as the molten sea, were vessels which contained water; but they were not of the same use with it. True, they were both to wash in; the sea to wash the worshippers, but the lavers to wash the sacrifice. 'He made the ten lavers to wash in them such things as they offered for the burnt-offering, but the sea *was* for the priests to wash in.'[2] 2. The burnt-offering was a type of the body of Christ, which he once offered for our sins; and the fire on which the sacrifice was burned, a type of the curse of the law which seized on Christ when he gave himself a ransom for us. For, therefore, that under the law was called the burnt-offering, because of the burning upon the altar.[3]

But what, then, must we understand by these lavers, and by this sacrifice being washed in them, in order to its being burned upon the altar?

I answer, Verily, I think that the ten lavers were a figure of the ten commandments; in the purity and perfection of Christ's obedience to which he became capable of being made a burnt-offering, acceptable to God for the sins of the people. Christ was made under the law, and all his acts of obedience to God for us were legal, and his living thus a perfect legal life was his washing his offering in these ten lavers, in order to his presenting it upon the altar for our sins. The lavers went upon wheels, to signify walking feet; and Christ walked in the law, and so became a clean offering to God for us. The wheels were of the very same as were the lavers, to show that Christ's obedience to the law was of the same, as to length and breadth, with its commands and demands to their utmost tittle and extent. The inwards and legs of the burnt offering were to be washed in these lavers,[4] to show that Christ should be pure and clean in heart and life.

We know that obedience, whether Christ's or ours, is called 'a walking in the way,' typified by the lavers walking upon their wheels. But I mean not by Christ, his washing of his offering, that he had any filthiness cleaving to his nature or obedience; yet this I say, that so far as our guilt laid upon him could impede, so far he wiped it off by washing in these lavers. For his

---

[1] 1 Kings 7:38.
[2] 2 Chronicles 4:6.
[3] Leviticus 6:9.
[4] Leviticus 1:9, 13; 2 Chronicles 4:6.

offering was to be without blemish, and without spot to God. Hence it is said, he sanctified himself in order to his suffering. 'And being made perfect, he became the author of eternal salvation unto all them that obey him.'[1]

For albeit he came holy into the world, yet that holiness was but preparatory to that by which he sanctified himself, in order to his suffering for sin. That, then, which was his immediate preparation for his suffering was his obedience to the law, his washing in these lavers. He, then, first yielded complete obedience to the law on our behalf, and then, as so qualified, offered his washed sacrifice for our sins without spot to God. Thus, therefore, he was our burnt-offering washed in the ten lavers, that he might, according to law, be accepted of the Lord.

And he set five of the lavers on the right side of the house, and five of them on the left. Thus were the ten divided, as the tables of the law, one showing our duty towards God, the other our duty towards our neighbour; in both which the burnt-offering was washed, that it might be clean in both respects. They might also be thus placed, the better to put the people in mind of the necessity of the sanction of Christ according to the law, in order to his offering of himself an offering to God for us.

XXXIX. OF THE TABLES IN THE TEMPLE.

'HE made also ten tables, and placed *them* in the temple, five on the right hand,[2] and five on the left.'[3]

Some, if not all of these tables, so far as I can see, were they on which the burnt-offering was to be cut in pieces, in order to its burning.

These tables were made of stone, of hewn stones, on which this work was done.[4] Now, since the burnt-offering was a figure of the body of Christ, the tables on which this sacrifice was slain must needs, I think, be a type of the heart, the stony heart, of the Jews. For had they not had hearts hard as an adamant, they could not have done that thing.

Upon these tables, therefore, was the death of Christ contrived,

---

[1] John 17:19; Hebrews 5:6–10.
[2] This is from the Genevan or puritan version. Our translation has 'on the right side.'—(OFFOR.)
[3] 2 Chronicles 4:8.
[4] Ezekiel 40:40–43.

and this horrid murder acted; even upon these tables of stone. In that they are called tables of hewn stone, it may be to show that all this cruelty was acted under smooth pretences, for hewn stones are smooth. The tables were finely wrought with tools, even as the heart of the Jews were with hypocrisy. But alas, they were *stone* still; that is, hard and cruel; else they could not have been an anvil for Satan to forge such horrid barbarism upon. The tables were in number the same with the lavers, and were set by them to show what are the fruits of being devoted to the law, as the Jews were, in opposition to Christ and his holy gospel. There flows nothing but hardness and a stony heart from thence. This was showed in its first writing; it was writ on tables of stone, figures of the heart of man; and on the same tables, or hearts, was the death of Jesus Christ compassed.

One would think that the meekness, gentleness, or good deeds of Jesus Christ might have procured in them some re-lentings when they were about to take away his life; but alas, their hearts were tables of stone! What feeling or compassion can a stone be sensible of? Here were stony hearts, stony thoughts, stony counsels, stony contrivances, a stony law, and stony hands; and what could be expected hence but barbarous cruelty indeed? 'If I ask *you*,' said Christ, 'ye will not answer me, nor let *me* go.'[1]

In that these stony tables were placed about the temple, it supposeth that they were temple-men, priests, scribes, rulers, lawyers, etc., that were to be the chief on whose hearts this murder was to be designed, and by them enacted to their own damnation without repentance.

XL. OF THE INSTRUMENTS WHEREWITH THIS SACRIFICE WAS SLAIN, AND OF THE FOUR TABLES THEY WERE LAID ON IN THE TEMPLE.

THE instruments that were laid upon the tables in the temple were not instruments of music, but those with which the burnt-offering was slain. 'And the four tables *were* of hewn stone for the burnt-offering: whereupon also they laid the instruments wherewith they slew the burnt-offering and the sacrifice.'[2]

Here we are to take notice that the tables are the same, and

---

[1] Luke 22:68.
[2] Ezekiel 40:42–43.

some of them of which we spake before. That the instruments
with which they slew the sacrifice were laid upon these tables.
The instruments with which they slew the sacrifices, what were
they but a bloody axe, bloody knives, bloody hooks, and bloody
hands? For these we need no proof; matter of fact declares it.
But what were those instruments a type of?

Answer. Doubtless they were a type of our sins. They were
the bloody axe, the knife, and bloody hands that shed his precious blood. They were the meritorious ones, without which he
could not have died. When I say ours, I mean the sins of the
world. Though, then, the hearts of the Jews were the immediate
contrivers, yet they were our sins that were the bloody tools or
instruments which slew the Son of God. 'He was wounded for
our transgressions, he died for our sins.'[1]

O the instruments of us churls, by which this poor man was
taken from off the earth![2] The whip, the buffetings, the crown of
thorns, the nails, the cross, the spear, with the vinegar and gall,
were all nothing in comparison of our sins. 'For the transgression of my people was he stricken.'[3] Nor were the flouts, taunts,
mocks, scorns, derisions, etc., with which they followed him from
the garden to the cross, such cruel instruments as these. They
were our sins then, our cursed sins, by, with, and for the sake of
which the Lord Jesus became a bloody sacrifice.

But why must the instruments be laid upon the tables?

1. Take the tables for the hearts of the murderers, and the
instruments for their sins, and what place more fit for such
instruments to be laid upon? It is God's command that these
things should be laid to heart, and he complains of those that do
not do it.[4]

2. Nor are men ever like to come to good, until these instruments with which the Son of God was slain indeed be laid to
heart. And they were eminently laid to heart even by them soon
after; the effect of which was the conversion of thousands of
them.[5]

3. Wherefore when it says these instruments must be laid upon

---

[1] Isaiah 53; 1 Corinthians 15; Galatians 1.
[2] Isaiah 32:7; Proverbs 30:14.
[3] Isaiah 53:8.
[4] Isaiah 42:25; 57:11.
[5] Acts 2:36–37.

the stony tables, he insinuates, that God would take a time to charge the murder of his Son home upon the consciences of them that did that murder, either to their conversion or condemnation. And is it not reason that they who did this horrid villany, should have their doings laid before their faces upon the tables of their heart? That they may look upon him whom they have pierced, and mourn.[1]

4. But these instruments were laid but upon some of the tables, and not upon all the ten, to show that not all, but some of those, so horrid, should find mercy of the Lord.

5. But we must not confine these tables only to the hearts of the bloody Jews; they were *our* sins for the which he died. Wherefore these instruments should be laid upon our tables too, and the Lord lay them there for good, that we also may see our horrid doings, and come bending to him for forgiveness!

6. These instruments thus lying on the tables in the temple, became a continual motive to God's people to repentance; for so oft as they saw these bloody and cruel instruments, they were put in mind how their sins should be the cause of the death of Christ.

7. It would be well also, if these instruments were at all times laid upon our tables, for our more humbling for our sins in every thing we do, especially upon the Lord's table, when we come to eat and drink before him. I am sure the Lord Jesus doth more than intimate, that he expects that we should do so, where he saith, When ye eat that bread, and drink that cup, do this in remembrance of me. In remembrance that I died for your sins, and consequently that they were the meritorious cause of the shedding of my blood.

To conclude. Let all men remember, that these cruel instruments are laid upon the table of their hearts, whether they see them there or no. 'The sin of Judah *is* written with a pen of iron, *and* with the point of a diamond . . . upon the table of their heart.'[2] A pen of iron will make letters upon a table made of stone, and the point of a diamond will make letters upon glass. Wherefore in this saying, God informs us that if we shall forbear to read these lines to our conversion, God will one day read them against us unto our condemnation.

---

[1] Zechariah 12:10; Revelation 1:7.
[2] Jeremiah 17:1.

XLI. OF THE CANDLESTICKS OF THE TEMPLE.

'AND he made ten candlesticks of gold, according to their form, and set *them* in the temple, five on the right hand, and five on the left.'[1]

These candlesticks were made of gold, to show the worth and value of them. They were made after the form, or exact, according to rule, like those that were made in the tabernacle, or according to the pattern which David gave to Solomon to make them by. Observe, there was great exactness in these; and need there was of this hint, that men might see that every thing will not pass for a right ordered candlestick with God.[2]

These candlesticks are said sometimes to be ten, sometimes seven, and sometimes one; ten here; seven,[3] and one in Zechariah 4.[4] Ten is a note of multitude, and seven a note of perfection, and one a note of unity. Now, as the precious stones with which the house was garnished were a type of ministerial gifts, so these candlesticks were a type of those that were to be the churches of the New Testament; wherefore he says, 'The candlesticks which thou sawest are the seven churches.'[5]

1. The candlesticks were here in number ten, to show that Christ under the New Testament would have a many gospel-churches. 'And I, if I be lifted up from the earth,' saith he, 'will draw all *men* unto me;' that is, abundance. For the children of the desolate, that is, of the New Testament church, shall be many more than they of the Jews were.[6]

2. In that the candlesticks were set by the lavers and stony tables, it might be to show us, that Christ's churches should be much in considering, that Christ, though he was righteous, yet died for our sins; though his life was according to the holy law,

---

[1] 2 Chronicles 4:7.

[2] Exodus 25:31–40; 1 Chronicles 28:15.

[3] Revelation 1:12–13.

[4] The candlesticks mentioned in 2 Chronicles 4:7, Zechariah 4, and Revelation 1, appear to have been of one pattern. A stem, with a bowl hearing a centre and six branches—three on each side. Of these there were ten in the temple. The prophets Zechariah and John, in their holy visions, saw but one, with its seven lamps secretly supplied by living olive trees. These lights 'are the eyes of the Lord, which run to and fro through the whole earth;' the seven lamps 'are the seven churches.' What a source for reflection is here opened.—(OFFOR.)

[5] Revelation 1:12–20.

[6] John 12:32; Galatians 4:27.

yet our stony hearts caused him to die. Yea, and that the candlesticks are placed there, it is to show us also, that we should be much in looking on the sins by which we caused him to die; for the candlesticks were set by those tables whereon they laid the instruments with which they slew the sacrifice.

3. These candlesticks being made according to form, seem not only to be exact as to fashion, but also as to work. For that in Exodus, with its furniture, was made precisely of one talent of gold, perhaps to show, that Christ's true spouse is not to be a grain more, nor a dram less, but just the number of God's elect. This is Christ's completeness, his fulness; one more, one less, would make his body a monster.

4. The candlestick was to hold the light, and to show it to all the house; and the church is to let her light so shine that they without may see the light.[1]

5. To this end the candlesticks were supplied with oil-olive, a type of the supply that the church hath, that her light may shine, even of the spirit of grace.

XLII. OF THE LAMPS BELONGING TO THE CANDLESTICKS OF THE TEMPLE.

To these candlesticks belonged several lamps, with their flowers and their knops.[2]

1. These lamps were types of that profession that the members of the church do make of Christ, whether such members have saving grace or not.[3]

2. These lamps were beautified with knops and flowers, to show how comely and beautiful that professor is, that adorns his profession with a suitable life and conversation.

3. We read that the candlestick in Zechariah had seven lamps belonging to it, and a bowl of golden oil[4] on the top; and that by golden pipes this golden oil emptied itself into the lamps, and all, doubtless, that the lamps might shine.[5]

4. Christ, therefore, who is the high-priest, and to whom it

---

[1] Matthew 5:15–16; Luke 8:16; 11:33; 12:35.

[2] Exodus 25:33; 2 Chronicles 4:21.

[3] Matthew 25:1–7.

[4] Oil called golden, from its representing that which, is better than thousands of gold and silver. So pure that, in the golden bowl, it would look like liquid gold.—(OFFOR.)

[5] Zechariah 4:2, 12.

belongs to dress the lamps, doth dress them accordingly. But now there are a lamp-carriers of two sorts; such as have only oil in their lamps, and such as have oil in their lamps and vessels too, and both these belong to the church, and in both these Christ will be glorified: and they should have their proper places at last. They that have the oil of grace in their hearts, as well as a profession of Christ in their hands, they shall go in with him to the wedding; but they who only make a profession, and have not oil in their vessels, will surely miscarry at last.[1]

5. Wherefore, O thou professor! thou lamp-carrier! have a care and look to thyself; content not thyself with that only that will maintain thee in a profession, for that may be done without saving grace. But I advise thee to go to Aaron, to Christ, the trimmer of our lamps, and beg thy vessel full of oil of him— that is, grace—for the seasoning of thy heart, that thou mayest have wherewith, not only to bear thee up now, but at the day of the bridegroom's coming, when many a lamp will go out, and many a professor be left in the dark; for that will to such be a woeful day.[2]

Some there are that are neither for lamps nor oil for themselves; neither are they pleased if they think they see it in others. But they that have lamps and they that have none, and they which would blow out other folk's light, must shortly appear to give an account of all their doings to God. And then they shall see what it is to have oil in their vessels and lamps: and what it is to be without in their vessels, though it is in their lamps; and what a dismal thing it is to be a malignant[3] to either; but at present let this suffice.

XLIII. OF THE SHEW-BREAD ON THE GOLDEN TABLE IN THE TEMPLE.

THERE was also shew-bread set upon a golden table in the temple.[4] The shew-bread consisted of twelve cakes made of fine

---

[1] Matthew 25.

[2] Leviticus 24:2; Matthew 25.

[3] A malignant was a term of reproach given to those who, in the civil wars, opposed Divine truth, and promoted popery and arbitrary domination. Clarendon calls it 'a term imposed upon those that the puritans wished to render odious to the people.'—(OFFOR.)

[4] 1 Kings 7:48.

flour, two tenth deals[1] were to go to one cake, and they were to be set in order in two rows upon the pure table.[2]

1. These twelve loaves to me do seem to be a type of the twelve tribes under the law, and of the children of God under the gospel, as they present themselves before God, in and by his ordinances through Christ. Hence the apostle says, 'For we *being* many are one bread,' etc.[3] For so were the twelve cakes, though twelve; and so are the gospel-saints, though many; for 'we, *being* many, are one body in Christ.'[4]

2. But they were a type of the true church, not of the false. For Ephraim, who was the head of the ten tribes in their apostacy, is rejected, as 'a cake not turned.' Indeed he is called a cake, as a false church may be called a church: but he is called 'a cake not turned,' as a false church is not prepared for God, nor fit to be set on the golden table before him.[5]

3. These cakes or shew-bread were to have frankincense strewed upon them, as they stood upon the golden table, which was a type of the sweet perfumes of the sanctifications of the Holy Ghost; to which I think Paul alludes, when he says, 'The offering up of the Gentiles might be acceptable' to God, 'being sanctified by the Holy Ghost.'[6]

4. They were to be set upon the pure table, new and hot; to show that God delighted in the company of new and warm believers. 'I remember thee, the kindness of thy youth:' 'when Israel *was* a child, then I loved him.'[7] Men at first conversion are like to a cake well baked, and new taken from the oven; they are warm, and cast forth a very fragrant scent, especially when, as warm, sweet incense is strewed upon them.

5. When the shew-bread was old and stale, it was to be taken away, and new and warm put in its place, to show that God has but little delight in the service of his own people when their duties grow stale and mouldy. Therefore he removed his old, stale, mouldy church of the Jews from before him, and set in

---

[1] A tenth deal is the tenth part of a Hebrew measure, called the ephah, containing about a bushel.—(OFFOR.)

[2] Leviticus 24:5–9.

[3] 1 Corinthians 10:17.

[4] Romans 12:5.

[5] Hosea 7:8.

[6] Romans 15:16.

[7] Jeremiah 2:2; Hosea 11:1.

their rooms upon the golden table the warm church of the Gentiles.

6. The shew-bread, by an often remove and renewing, was continually to all them before the Lord in his house, to show us, that always, as long as ordinances shall be of use, God will have a new, warm, and sanctified people to worship him.

7. Aaron and his sons were to eat the old shew-bread, to show that when saints have lived in the world as long as living is good for them, and when they can do no more service for God in the world, they shall yet be accepted of Jesus Christ; and that it shall be as meat and drink to him to save them from all their unworthinesses.

8. The new shew-bread was to be set even on the Sabbath before the Lord, to show with what warmth of love and affections God's servants should approach his presence upon his holy day.

XLIV. OF THE SNUFFERS BELONGING TO THE CANDLESTICKS AND LAMPS OF THE TEMPLE.

As there were candlesticks and lamps, so there were snuffers also prepared for these in the temple of the Lord. 'And the snuffers were snuffers of gold.'[1] 1. Snuffers. The use of snuffers is to trim the lamps and candles, that their lights may shine the brighter. 2. Snuffers, you know, are biting, pinching things; but use them well, and they will prove not only beneficial to those within the house, but profitable to the lights.

Snuffers, you may say, of what were they a type?

Answer. If our snuffs are our superfluities of naughtiness, our snuffers then are those righteous reproofs, rebukes, and admonitions, which Christ has ordained to be in his house for good; or, as the apostle hath it, for our edification; and perhaps Paul alludes to these when he bids Titus to rebuke the Cretians sharply, that they might be sound in the faith.[2] As who should say, they must use the snuffers of the temple to trim their lights withal, if they burn not well. These snuffers therefore are of great use in the temple of God; only, as I said, they must be used wisely. It is not for every fool to handle snuffers at or about the candles, lest perhaps, instead of mending the light, they put the candle out. And therefore Paul bids

---

[1] 1 Kings 7:50.
[2] Titus 1:12–13.

them that are spiritual do it.[1] My reason tells me, that if I use these snuffers as I should, I must not only endeavour to take the superfluous snuff away, but so to do it, that the light thereby may be mended; which then is done if, as the apostle saith, I use sharp-ness to edification, and not for destruction.[2]

Are not the seven churches in Asia called by name of candle-sticks? And why candlesticks, if they were not to hold the candles? And candles must have snuffers therewith to trim the lights. And Christ, who is our true Aaron, in those rebukes which he gave those churches, alluding to these snuffers, did it that their lights might shine the brighter.[3] Wherefore, as he used them, he did it still with caution to their light, that it might not be impaired. For as he still thus trimmed these lamps, he yet encouraged what he saw would shine if helped. He only nipt the snuff away.

Thus, therefore, he came to them with these snuffers in his hand, and trimmed their lamps and candlesticks.[4] This should teach ministers, to whom it belongs under Christ to use the snuffers well. Strike at the snuff, not at the light, in all your rebukes and admonitions; snuff not your lamps of a private revenge, but of a design to nourish grace and gifts in churches. Thus our Lord himself says he did, in his using of these snuffers about these candlesticks. 'As many,' saith he, 'as I love, I rebuke and chasten; be zealous therefore, and repent.'[5]

To conclude; Watchman, watch, and let not your snuffs be too long, nor pull them off with your fingers, or carnal reasonings, but with godly admonitions, etc. Use your snuffers graciously, curb vice, nourish virtue; so you will use them well, and so your light will shine to the glory of God.[6]

---

[1] Galatians 6:1.

[2] 1 Corinthians 5:4–5; 2 Corinthians 13:10.

[3] Revelation 2 & 3.

[4] Revelation 2:4, 20; 3:2, 15.

[5] Revelation 3:19.

[6] Daniel Burgess published a curious sermon, in 1697, on the golden snuffers, showing that they are a type or emblem of spiritual snuffing or reproving; and of pure gold, to show that reprovers should be holy and unblameable. His directions and cautions are valuable, but Bunyan says much more in his few lines than Burgess does in his eighty pages.—(OFFOR.)

XLV. OF THE SNUFF-DISHES THAT WERE WITH THE SNUFFERS IN THE TEMPLE.

As there were snuffers, so there were also snuff-dishes in the temple; 'and they were also made of gold.'[1] The snuff-dishes were those in which the snuffs were put when snuffed off, and by which they were carried forth of the temple. They therefore, as the snuffers are, are of great use in the temple of God. 1. By them the golden floor of the temple is kept from being daubed by the snuffs. 2. By them also the clean hands of those that worship there are kept from being defiled. 3. By them also the stinks of the snuffs are soonest suppressed in the temple; and consequently the tender noses of them that worship there preserved from being offended.

Snuffs, you know, are daubing things, stinking things, nauseous things; therefore we must take heed that they touch not this floor on which we walk, nor defile the hands which we lift up to God, when we come to worship him. But how must this be done, but as we take them off with the snuffers, and put them in these snuff-dishes? Some are for being at the snuffs with their fingers, and will also cast them at their feet, and daub the floor of God's holy house; but usually such do burn as well as defile themselves. But is it not a shame for a man to defile himself with that vice which he rebuketh in another? Let us then, while we are taking away the snuffs of others, hate even the garment spotted by the flesh, and labour to carry such stink with the snuff dishes out of the temple of God.

Snuff-dishes, you may say, what are they?

I answer, If sins are the snuffs, and rebukes and admonitions the snuffers; then, methinks, repentance, or, in case that be wanting, the censures of the church, should be the snuff-dishes. Hence, repentance is called a church-cleansing grace, and the censures of the church a purging out of the old leaven, and making it a new lump.[2]

Ah! were these snuff-dishes more of use in the churches, we should not have this man's snuff defile that man's fingers as it doth. Nor would the temple of God be so besmeared with these snuffs, and be daubed as it is.

---

[1] Exodus 25:38; 37:23; Numbers 4:9.
[2] 1 Corinthians 5:2; 2 Corinthians 7:11.

Ah! snuffs pulled off, lie still in the temple-floor, and there stink, and defile both feet and fingers, both the callings and conversations of temple-worshippers, to the disparaging of religion, and the making of religious worship but of low esteem with men; and all, I say, for want of the due use of these snuffers, and these snuff-dishes, there. Nay, are not whole churches now defiled with those very snuffs, that long since were plucked off, and all for want of the use of these snuff-dishes, according to the Lord's commandment. For you must know, that reproof and admonitions are but of small use, where repentance, or church-censures, are not thereto annexed. When ministers use the snuffers, the people should hold the snuff-dishes.

Round reproofs for sin, when they light upon penitent hearts, then brave work is in the church: then the snuff is not only pulled away, but carried out of the temple of God aright, etc. And now the worship and worshippers shine like gold. 'As an ear-ring of gold, and an ornament of fine gold, *so is* a wise reprover upon an obedient ear.'[1]

Ministers, it appertains to you to use the snuffers, and to teach the people to hold the snuff-dishes right.[2] We must often be snuffed with these snuffers, or our light will burn but dimly, our candle will also waste. Pray, therefore, O men of God, look diligently to your people. Snuff them as you see there is need; but touch not their snuff with your white fingers; a little smutch on YOU will be seen a great way. Remember also that you leave them nowhere, but with these snuff-dishes, that the temple may be cleared of them. Do with the snuff as the neat housewife doth with the toad which she finds in her garden. She takes the fork, or a pair of tongs, and therewith doth throw it over the pales. Cast them away, I say, with fear, zeal, care, revenge, and with great indignation, and then your church, your conversation, your fingers, and all, will be kept white and clean.[3]

XLVI. OF THE GOLDEN TONGS BELONGING TO THE TEMPLE.

THERE were also tongs of gold used in the temple of old.[4] 1.

---

[1] Proverbs 25:12.
[2] Acts 20:20–21; 2 Timothy 4:2.
[3] 2 Corinthians 7:11.
[4] 1 Kings 7:49.

These tongs were used about the altar, to order the fire there. 2.
They were used too about the candlestick, and are therefore
called HIS tongs. 3. Perhaps there were tongs for both these
services; but of that the word is silent.

But what were they used about the candlestick to do?

Answer. To take holy fire from off the altar to light the lamps
withal. For the fire of the temple was holy fire, such as at first
was kindled from heaven, and when kindled, maintained by the
priests, and of that the lamps were lighted.[1] Nor was there,
upon pain of death, any other fire to be used there.[2] These tongs,
therefore, were used to take fire from off the altar to light the
lamps and candlesticks withal. For to trim the lights, and to
dress the lamps, was Aaron's work day by day. He shall light
and order the lamps upon the pure candlestick before the Lord,
and Aaron did so. He lighted the seven lamps thereof, as the
Lord commanded Moses.[3] What is a lamp or candlestick to us, if
there be not light thereon; and how lighted without fire, and
how shall we take up coals to light the lamps withal, if we have
not tongs prepared for that purpose? With these tongs fire also
was taken from off the altar, and put into the censers to burn
sweet incense with, before the Lord. The tongs then were of
great use in the temple of the Lord.

But what were the tongs a type of?

The altar was a type of Christ; the fire of the Holy Ghost; and
these tongues were a type of that holy hand of God's grace, by
which the coals, or several dispensations and gifts of the Holy
Ghost, are taken and given to the church, and to her members,
for her work and profit in this world.

Tongs, we know, are used instead of fingers; wherefore
Aaron's golden tongs were a type of Christ's golden fingers.[4]
Isaiah saith that one of the seraphims flew to him with 'a live
coal in his hand, *which* he had taken with the tongs from off the
altar.' Here the type and antitype, to wit, tongs and hand, are
put together.[5] But the prophet Ezekiel, treating of like matters,
quite waives the type, the tongs, and speaketh only of this holy

---

[1] Leviticus 9:24; 2 Chronicles 7:1.

[2] Leviticus 10:1–2.

[3] Exodus 10:24–25; Leviticus 24:2–3; Numbers 8:3.

[4] Song of Solomon 5:14.

[5] Isaiah 6:6.

hand; 'And he spake unto the man clothed with linen, and said, Go in between the wheels under the cherub'—where the mercy-seat stood, where God dwelt;[1]—'and fill thy hand with coals of fire from between the cherubims.'[2]

Thus you see our golden tongs are now turned into a golden hand; into the golden hand of the man clothed in linen, which is Jesus Christ, who at his ascension received of God the Father the Spirit in all fulness, to give, as his divine wisdom knew was best, the several coals or dispensations thereof unto his church, for his praise, and her edification.[3] It is by this hand also that this holy fire is put into our censers. It is this hand also that takes this coal, therewith to touch the lips of ministers, that their words may warm like fire; and it is by this hand that the Spirit is given to the churches, as returns of their holy prayers.[4]

It was convenient that the fire in the temple should be disposed of by golden tongs; but the Holy Ghost, by the golden hand of Christ's grace, for that can wittingly dispose of it, according as men and things are placed, and to do and be done in the churches; wherefore he adds, 'And *one* cherub stretched forth his hand from between the cherubims, unto the fire that *was* between the cherubims, and took *thereof*, and put *it* into the hands of *him that was* clothed with linen, who took *it* and went out.'[5]

By this hand, then, by this Man's hand, the coals of the altar are disposed of, both to the lamps, the candlesticks, the censers, and the lips of ministers, according to his own good pleasure. And of all this were the tongs in the temple a type.

XLVII. OF THE ALTAR OF INCENSE IN THE TEMPLE.

THE altar of incense was made first for the tabernacle, and that of shittim wood; but it was made for the temple of cedar, and it was to be set before the veil, that is, by the ark of the testimony, before the mercy-seat; that is, at the entering of the holiest, but not within. And the priest was to approach it every morning,

---

[1] Exodus 25; Psalm 80:1.
[2] Ezekiel 10:2.
[3] Matthew 3:11; Acts 2.
[4] Luke 11:9–13; Romans 8:26; Revelation 8:5.
[5] Ezekiel 10:7.

which, as to the holiest, he might not do. Besides, when he went in to make an atonement, he was to take fire from off that altar to burn his incense within the holy place.[1]

1. It was called the *golden altar*, because it was overlaid with pure gold. This altar was not for burnt-offering, as the brazen altar was; nor for the meat-offering, nor the drink-offering, but to burn incense thereon.[2] Which sweet incense was a type of grace and prayer.[3]

2. Incense, or that called incense here, was not a simple but a compound, made up of sweet spices called *stacte*, *onycha*, and *galbanum*; and these three, may answer to these three parts of this duty, to wit, prayer, supplication, and intercession.[4]

3. This incense was to be burned upon the altar every morn-ing; upon that altar which was called the altar of incense, which was before the veil; to show that it is our duty every morning to make our prayer to God by Jesus Christ before the veil; that is, before the door of heaven, and there to seek, knock, and ask for what we need, according to the word.[5]

4. This incense was to be kindled every morning, to show how HE continueth interceding for us, and also that all true praise of men to God is by the work, the renewed work, of the Holy Ghost upon our hearts.[6]

5. Incense, as you see, was made of sweet spices, such as were gummy, and so apt to burn with a smoke, to show, that not cold and flat, but hot and fervent, is the prayer that flows from the spirit of faith and grace.[7]

6. The smoke of this incense was very sweet and savoury, like pleasant perfume, to show how delightful and acceptable the very sound and noise of right prayer is unto the nostrils of the living God, because it comes from a broken heart.[8]

7. This incense was to be offered upon the golden altar, to show us that no prayer is accepted but what is directed to God

---

[1] Exodus 30:1–10; Leviticus 16:18.
[2] Exodus 30:7.
[3] Psalm 141:2.
[4] Exodus 30:34–37; 37:29; 1 Timothy 2:1.
[5] Luke 11:9–13.
[6] Romans 8:26.
[7] Zechariah 12:10; Jeremiah 5:16.
[8] Psalm 51:17; Song of Solomon 2:14.

in the name of his holy and blessed Son our Saviour.[1]

8. They were commanded to burn incense every morning upon this altar, to show that God is never weary of the godly prayers of his people. It also showeth that we need every day to go to God for fresh supplies of grace to carry us through this evil world.

9. This altar, though it stood without the veil, to teach us to live by faith, and to make use of the name of Christ, as we find it recorded in the first temple, yet was placed so nigh unto the holiest, that the smell of the smoke might go in thither; to show that it is not distance of place that can keep the voice of true prayer from our God, the God of heaven; but that he will be taken with what we ask for according to his word. It stood, I say, nigh the veil, nigh the holiest; and he that burnt incense there, did make his approach to God. Hence the Psalmist, when he spake of praying, saith, 'It is good for me to draw near to God.'[2]

10. This altar thus placed did front the ark within the veil; to put us in mind that the law is kept therein from hurting us; to let us know also that the mercy-seat is above, upon the ark, and that God doth sit thereon, with his pardon in his hand to save us. O! what speaking thing's are types, shadows, and parables, had we but eyes to see, had we but ears to hear! He that did approach the altar with incense of old aright—and then he did so when he approached it by Aaron, his high-priest—pleased God; how much more shall we have both person and prayers accepted, and a grant of what we need, if indeed we come as we should to God by Jesus Christ. But take heed you approach not to a wrong altar; take heed also that you come not with strange fire; for they are dangerous things, and cause the worshippers to miss of what they would enjoy. But more of this in the next particular.

XLVIII. OF THE GOLDEN CENSERS
BELONGING TO THE TEMPLE.

THERE were also golden censers belonging to the temple, and they were either such as belonged to the sons of Levi in general, or that were for Aaron and his sons in special.[3] The censers of

---

[1] 1 Peter 2:5; Hebrews 13:15.

[2] Psalm 73:28; Hebrews 10:22.

[3] Numbers 16:6, 17–18.

the Levites were a type of ours; but the censer of Aaron was a
type of Christ's. The censers, as was hinted before, were for this
use in the temple, namely, to hold the holy fire in, on which
incense was to be burned before the Lord.[1]

These censers then were types of hearts. Aaron's golden one
was a type of Christ's golden heart, and the censers of the Levites
were types of other worshippers' hearts. The fire also which was
put therein was a type of that Spirit by which we pray, and the
incense that burnt thereon, a type of our desires. Of Christ's
censer we read, Revelations the eighth, which is always filled
with much incense; that is, with continual intercessions, which he
offereth to God for us; and from whence also there always goes a
cloud of sweet savour, covering the mercy-seat.[2]

But to speak of the censers, and fire, and incense of the worshippers; for albeit they were all put under one rule, that is, to
be according to law, yet oftentimes, as were the worshippers,
such were the censers, fire, and incense. 1. Hence the two
hundred and fifty censers with which Korah and his company
offered, are called the censers of sinners; for they came with
wicked hearts then to burn incense before the Lord.[3] 2. Again, as
the censers of these men were called the censers of sinners,
showing they came at that time to God with naughty hearts, so
the fire that was in Nadab and Abihu's censers is called strange
fire, which the Lord commanded them not.[4] 3. This strange fire
was a type of that strange spirit opposed to the Spirit of God, in
and by which, notwithstanding, some adventure to perform
worship to God. 4. Again, as these censers are called the censers
of sinners, and this fire called strange fire, so the incense of such
is also called strange, and is said to be an abomination unto
God.[5]

Thus you see that both the censers, fire, and incense of some
is rejected, even as the heart, spirit, and prayer of sinners are
an abomination unto God.[6]

But there were besides these true censers, holy fire and sweet

---

[1] Leviticus 10:1–2.

[2] Leviticus 16:13; Hebrews 7:25; Revelation 8:3–4.

[3] Numbers 16:17, 37.

[4] Leviticus 10:1.

[5] Exodus 30:9; Isaiah 1:13; 66:3.

[6] Hosea 7:14; 4:12; 5:4; Proverbs 28:9.

incense among the worshippers in the temple, and their service was accepted by Aaron their high-priest; for that was through the faith of Christ, and these were a type of our true gospel worshippers, who come with holy hearts, the holy spirit, and holy desires before their God, by their Redeemer. These are a perfume in his nose. 'The prayer of the upright *is* his delight.'[1] Their prayers went up like 'incense, *and* the lifting up of their hands *as* the evening sacrifice.'[2]

Let them then that pretend to worship before God in his holy temple look to it, that both their censers, fire, and incense, heart, spirit, and desires, be such as the word requires; lest, instead of receiving of gracious returns from the God of heaven, their censers be laid up against them; lest the fire of God devours them, and their incense become an abomination to him, as it happened to those made mention of before.

But it is said the censers of Korah and his company was hallowed.

Answer. So is God's worship, which is so his by his ordination, yet even that very worship may be spoiled by man's transgression. Prayer is God's ordinance, but all prayer is not accepted of God. We must then distinguish between the thing commanded, and our using of that thing. The temple was God's house, but was abused by the irreverence of those that worshipped there, even to the demolishing of it.

A golden censer is a gracious heart, heavenly fire is the Holy Ghost, and sweet incense the effectual fervent prayer of faith. Have you these? These God expects, and these you must have if ever your persons or performances be of God accepted.

XLIX. OF THE GOLDEN SPOONS OF THE TEMPLE.

1. The golden spoons belonging to the temple were in number, according to Moses, twelve; answering to the twelve tribes.[3] But when the temple was built, I suppose they were more, because of the number of the basons.

2. The spoons, as I suppose, were for the worshippers in the temple to eat that broth withal, wherein the trespass-offerings were boiled: for which purpose there were several cauldrons

---

[1] Proverbs 15:8.

[2] Psalm 141:2.

[3] Numbers 7:86.

hanged in the corners of that court called the priest's to boil
them in.[1]

3. Now, in that he saith here were spoons, what is it but that
there are also babes in the temple of the Lord. There was broth
for babes as well as meat for men, and spoons to eat the broth
withal.

4. True, the gospel being more excellent than the law, doth
change the term, and instead of broth, saith, There is milk for
babes. But in that he saith milk, he insinuates there are spoons
for children in the church.

5. 'I could not,' saith Paul to them at Corinth, 'speak to you as
unto spiritual, but as unto carnal, *even* as unto babes in Christ. I
have fed you with milk and not with meat; for hitherto ye were
not able to *bear it*, neither yet now are ye able.'[2]

6. See, here were need of spoons, milk is spoon meat; for here
were those which could not feed themselves with milk, let them
then that are men eat the strong meat. 'For every one that useth
milk *is* unskilful in the word of righteousness, for he is a babe.
But strong meat belongeth to them that are of full age, *even*
those who, by reason of use, have their senses exercised to
discern both good and evil.'[3]

7. Spoons, you know, are to feed us with weak and thin food,
even with that which best suiteth with weak stomachs, or with a
babyish temper. Hence, as the strong man is opposed to the
weak, so the milk is opposed to the strong meat.

8. So then, though the babe in Christ is weaker than the man
in Christ, yet is he not by Christ left unprovided for; for here is
milk for babes, and spoons to eat it with. All this is taught us by
the spoons; for what need is there of spoons where there is
nothing to eat but strong meat?

9. Babes, you know, have not only babyish stomachs, but also
babyish tricks, and must be dealt withal as babes; their childish
talk and frompered carriages must be borne withal.

10. Sometimes they cry for nothing, yea, and count them for
their foes which rebuke their childish toys and ways. All which
the church must bear, because they are God's babes; yea, they
must feed them too: for if he has found them milk and spoons, it

---

[1] 1 Samuel 2:13–14; Ezekiel 46:19–20.
[2] 1 Corinthians 3:1–2.
[3] Hebrews 5:13–14.

is that they may be fed therewith, and live: yea, grown ministers are God's nurses, wherefore they must have a lap to lay
them in, and knees to dandle them upon, and spoons to feed
them with.[1]

11. Nor are the babes but of use in the church of God; for he
commands that they may be brought to cry with the congregation before the Lord for mercy for the land.[2]

12. Incense, I told you, was a type of prayers, and the spoons,
in the time of Moses, were presented at the temple full of it.
Perhaps to show that God will, with the milk which he has
provided for them, give it to them as a return of their crying to
him, even as the nurse gives the child the teat and milk.

13. You know the milk is called for when the child is crying,
as we say, to stop its mouth with it. O babes! did you but cry
soundly, God would give you yet more milk.

14. But what were these golden spoons a type of? I answer, if
the milk is the juice and consolations of the Word, then the
spoons must be those soft sentences and golden conclusions with
which the ministers feed their souls by it, 'I have fed you,' saith
Paul, 'with the milk of the Word;' saith Peter, 'even as you have
been able to bear it.' Compare these two or three texts—1 Peter
2:1–3; 1 Corinthians 3:2; 1 Thessalonians 2:7.

15. And this is the way to strengthen the weak hands, and to
confirm the feeble knees. This is the way to make them grow to
be men who now are but as infants of days. 'Thus a little one
shall become a thousand, and a small one a strong nation.' Yea,
thus in time you may make a little child to jostle it with a
leopard; yea, to take a lion by the beard; yea, thus you may
embolden him to put his hand to the hole of the asp, and to play
before the den of the cockatrice.[3]

Who is most stout was once a babe; he that can now eat meat

---

[1] Great was the fatherly care felt by Bunyan for his own children, especially for his blind Mary; and judging by the lessons he draws from the
temple spoons, those feelings extended to his church. It must be a
severe trial to a minister's temper, when teased with babes in religion
at three score and ten years of age, especially if they are old professors.
Thus Bunyan, in addressing the readers of his emblems, says—

'We now have boys with beards, and girls that be
'Huge as old women wanting gravity.'—(OFFOR.)

[2] Joel 2:16.

[3] Isaiah 11:6–8; 60:22.

was sometimes glad of milk, and to be fed with the spoon. Babes in Christ, therefore, must not be despised nor overlooked; God has provided them milk and spoons to eat it with, that they may grow up to be men before him.

L. OF THE BOWLS AND BASONS BELONGING TO THE TEMPLE.

As there were spoons, so there were bowls and basons belonging to the temple. Some of these were of gold, and some of silver; and when they were put together, their number was four hundred and forty. These you read of.[1] The bowls or basons were not to wash in, as was the sea and lavers of the temple; they were rather to hold the messes in, which the priests at their holy feasts did use to set before the people. This being so, they were types of that proportion of faith by which, or by the measure of which, every man received of the holy food for the nourishment of his soul. For, as a man, had he a thousand messes set before him, he eating for his health, cannot go beyond what his stomach will bear; so neither can the child of God, when he comes to worship in the temple of God, receive of the good things that are there, beyond the 'proportion of his faith.'[2] Or, as it is in another place, according to 'the ability which God giveth.'[3] And hence it is, at the self-same ordinance, some receive three times as much as others do; for that their bowl, I mean their faith, is able to receive it. Yea, Benjamin's mess was five times as big as was the mess of any of his brethren; and so it is with some saints while they eat with their brother Joseph in the house of the living God.

There are three go to the same ordinance, and are all of them believers; who, when they come home, and compare notes, do find their receivings are not of the same quantity. One says, I got but little; the other says, It was a pretty good ordinance to me; the third says, I was exceeding well there. Why, to be sure, he that had but little there, had there but little faith; for great faith in him would have received more. He had it then according to the largeness of his bowl, even according to his faith, 'as God hath dealt to every man the measure of faith.'[4] Mark, faith is a

---

[1] Ezra 1:10.
[2] Romans 12:6.
[3] 1 Peter 4:11.
[4] Romans 12:3.

certain measure, and that not only as to its degree, but for that it can receive, retain, or hold what is put into it.

So then, here it is no matter how much milk or holy broth there is; but how big is thy bowl, thy faith. Little bowls hold but little, nor canst thou receive but as thy faith will bear; I speak now of God's ordinary dealing with his people, for so he saith in his Word, 'According to your faith be it unto you.'[1] If a man goeth to the ocean sea for water, let him carry but an egg-shell with him, and with that he shall not bring a gallon home. I know, indeed, that our little pots have a promise of being made like the bowls of the altar; but still our mess must be according to our measure, be that small, or be it great. The same prophet saith again, the saints shall be 'filled like bowls, *and* as the corners of the altar;' which, though it supposes an enlargement, yet it must be confined to that measure of faith which is provided for its reception.[2] And suppose these bowls should signify the promises, though the saints, not the promises, are compared to them, because they, not promises, are the subjects of faith; yet it is the promise by our measure of faith in that, that is nourishing to our souls.

When Ahasuerus made a feast to his subjects, they drank their wine in bowls. They did not drink it by the largeness of the vessel whence they drew it, but according to their health, and as their stomachs would so receive it.[3] Thy faith, then, is one of the bowls or basons of the temple, by, or according to which, thou receivest thy mess, when thou sittest feasting at the table of God. And observe, all the bowls were not made of gold, as all faith is not of a saving sort. It is the golden faith that is right; the silver bowls were of an inferior sort.[4]

Some, I say, have golden faith; all faith is not so. Wherefore look to it, soul, that thy bowl, thy faith, be golden faith, or of the best kind. Look, I say, after a good faith, and great, for a great faith receives a great mess. Of old, beggars did use to carry their bowls in their laps, when they went to a door for an alms.[5]

---

[1] Matthew 9:29.

[2] Zechariah 9:15; 14:20.

[3] Esther 1:7–8.

[4] Revelation 3:18.

[5] The degraded state of the poor, when the religious houses (so called) distributed food to all comers, was long felt after the suppression of those hot-beds of vice, from the encouragement they gave to idleness, pauperism, and the most vicious habits. Even in Bunyan's days the

Footnotes are continued on the next page.

Consequently, if their bowls were but little, they ofttimes came off by the loss, though the charity of the giver was large. Yea, the greater the charity, the larger the loss, because the beggar's bowl was too little. Mark it well, it is ofttimes thus in the mat ters of our God. Art thou a beggar, a beggar at God's door, be sure thou gettest a great bowl; for as thy bowl is, so will be thy mess. 'According to your faith,' saith he, 'be it unto you.'[1]

LI. OF THE FLAGONS AND CUPS OF THE TEMPLE.

THE next thing to be considered is the flagons and cups of the temple; of these we read.[2] These were of great use among the Jews, especially on their feasting days; as of their sabbaths, new-moons, and the like.[3]

For instance, the day that David danced before the ark, 'he dealt among all the people, *even* among the whole multitude of Israel, as well to the women as men, to every one a cake of bread, and a good piece *of flesh*, and a flagon *of wine*.'[4] 'In this mountain,' that is, in the temple typically, saith the prophet, 'shall the Lord of hosts make unto all people a feast of fat things, a feast of wines on the lees, of fat things full of marrow, of wines on the lees well refined.'[5]

These are feasting times; the times in which our Lord used to have his spouse into his wine-cellar, and in which he used to display with delight his banner over her head in love.[6] The church of Christ, alas! is of herself a very sickly puely thing; a woman; a weaker vessel; but how much more must she needs be so weak, when the custom of women is upon her, or when she is sick of love? Then she indeed has need of a draught, for she now sinks, and will not else be supported. 'Stay me with flagons,'

Footnotes are continued from the last page.

beggar, carrying a bowl to receive the fruit of their industrious neighbours' toil, was still remembered. At intervals, plague and famine swept away the helpless wretches, to the terror of all classes. How severely is this curse still felt in Ireland.—(OFFOR.)

[1] Matthew 9:29.

[2] 1 Chronicles 28:17; Jeremiah 52:19; Isaiah 22:24.

[3] Leviticus 23:13; Numbers 28:7; 1 Chronicles 16:3; Isaiah 25:6; 62:8–9.

[4] 2 Samuel 6:19; 1 Chronicles 16:3.

[5] Isaiah 25:6.

[6] Song of Solomon 2:4–5.

saith she, 'and comfort me with apples, for I *am* sick of love.'[1]

These flagons, therefore, were types of those feastings, and of those large draughts of Divine love, that the Lord Jesus draweth for and giveth to his spouse in those days that he feasteth with them. For then he saith, 'Drink, yea, drink abundantly, O beloved.' This he does to cheer her up under her hours of sadness and dejection; for now new 'corn shall make the young men cheerful, and new wine the maids.'[2]

As there were flagons, so there were cups; and they are called cups of consolation, and cups of salvation, because, as I said, they were they by which God at his feastings with his people, or when he suppeth with them, giveth out the more large draughts of his love unto his saints, to revive the spirits of the humble, and to revive the hearts of the contrite ones. At these times God made David's cup run over. For we are now admitted, if our faith will bear it, to drink freely into this grace, and to be merry with him.[3] This is that to which the apostle alludeth, when he saith, 'Be not drunk with wine, wherein is excess, but be filled with the Spirit; speaking to yourselves in psalms, and hymns, and spiritual songs, singing and making melody in your heart unto the Lord.'[4]

For the cups, as to their use in the general, understand them as of the bowls made mention of before. For assurances are the blooms and flowers of faith, not always on it, though usually on feasting days it is so. So the degree of the one is still according to the measure of the other.[5]

LII. OF THE CHARGERS OF THE TEMPLE.

IN the tabernacle they had but twelve of them, and they were made of silver; but in the temple they had in all a thousand and thirty. The thirty were made of gold, the rest were made of silver.[6] These chargers were not for uses common or profane,

---

[1] Song of Solomon 2:5.

[2] Proverbs 31:6–7; Psalm 116:13; Jeremiah 16:7; Song of Solomon 5; Zechariah 9:17.

[3] Psalm 23:5; Luke 15:22–24; Song of Solomon 5:1; 7:11–12; John 14:23; Revelation 3:20.

[4] Ephesians 5:18–19.

[5] James 5; Romans 15:13.

[6] Ezra 1:9; Numbers 7:84.

but, as I take it, they were those in which the passover, and other meat-offerings, were drest up, when the people came to eat before God in his holy temple. The meat, you know, I told you, was opposite to milk; and so are these chargers to the bowls, and cups, and flagons of the temple.

The meat was of two sorts, roast or boiled. Of that which was roasted was the passover, and of that which was boiled were the trespass-offerings. Wherefore, concerning the passover, he saith, 'Eat not of it raw, nor sodden at all with water, but roast *with* fire; his head with his legs, and with the purtenance thereof.'[1] This roast meat was a type of the body of Christ as suffering for our sins, the which, when it was roast, was, and is as dressed up in chargers, and set before the congregations of the saints.

But what were the chargers a type of? I also ask, in what charger our gospel passover is now dressed up and set before the people? Is it not in the four evangelists, the prophets, and epistles of the apostles? They therefore are the chargers and the ordinance of the supper; in these also are the trespass-offerings, with what is fried in pans, mystically prepared for the children of the Highest.

And why might they not be a type of gospel sermons?

I answer, I think not so fitly; for, alas! the best of sermons in the world are but as thin slices cut out of those large dishes. Our ministers are the carvers, good doctrine is the meat, and the chargers in which this meat is found are the holy canonical Scriptures, etc., though, as I said, most properly the New Testament of our Lord and Saviour Jesus Christ.

In these is Christ most truly, lively, and amply set before us as crucified, or roasted at the fire of God's law for our sins, that we might live by him through faith, feeding upon him.[2]

There is in these chargers not only meat, but sauce, if you like it, to eat the meat withal; for the passover there are bitter herbs, or sound repentance; and for other, as the thank-offerings, there is holy cheerfulness and prayers to God for grace. All these are set forth before in the holy Scriptures, and presented to us thereby, as in the gold chargers of the temple. He that will scoff at this, let him scoff. The chargers were a type

---

[1] Exodus 12:9.

[2] 2 Corinthians 3:12; Galatians 3:12; Acts 3:18–22; 13:2–5; 26:22; 1 Peter 1:10; Acts 7:52; 15:15; 28:23; Romans 16:26; Revelation 10:7.

of something; and he that can show a fitter antitype than is here proposed to consideration, let him do it, and I will be thankful to him.

Christians, here is your meat before you, and get your carvers to slice it out for you, and this know, the deeper you dip it in the sauce, the better it will relish. But let not unbelief teach you such manners as to make you leave the best bits behind you. For your liberty is to eat freely of the best, of the fat, and of the sweet.

LIII. OF THE GOINGS OUT OF THE TEMPLE.

As to the comings into the temple, of them we have spoken already; namely, of the outer and inner court, as also of the doors of the porch and temple. The coming in was but one strait course, and that a type of Jesus Christ; but the goings out were many.[1]

Now, as I said, it is insinuated that the goings out are many, answerable to the many ways which the children of men have invented to apostatize in from God. Christ is the way into; but sin the way out of the temple of God. True, I read not of a description of the goings out of this house, as I read of the comings in. Only when they had Athaliah out thence, she is said to go out by the way by which the horses come into the king's stables, and there she was slain, as it were upon the horse dung-hill.[2] When Uzziah also went out of this house for his transgression, he was cast out of all society, and made to dwell in a kind of a pest-house, even to the day of his death.[3]

Thus, therefore, though these goings out are not particularly described, the judgments that followed them that have for their transgressions been thrust out thence, have been both remarkable and tremendous: for to die upon a dung-hill, or in a pest-house, and that for wicked actions, is a shameful, a disgraceful thing. And God will still be spreading dung upon the faces of such; no greatness shall prevent it.[4] Yea, and will take them away with it. 'I will drive them out of my house,' says he, 'I will love them no more.'[5]

But what are we to understand in gospel days, by going out of

---

[1] John 10:9; 14:6.

[2] 2 Kings 11:16; 2 Chronicles 23:15.

[3] 2 Chronicles 26:21.

[4] Malachi 2:3.

[5] Hosea 9:15.

the house of the Lord, for or by sin? I answer, if it be done
voluntarily, then sin leads you out: if it be done by the holy
compulsion of the church, then it is done by the judicial judgment of God; that is, they are cut off, and cast out from thence,
as a just reward for their transgressions.[1,2]

Well, but whither do they go, that are thus gone out of the
temple or church of God? I answer, not to the dunghill with
Athaliah, nor to the pest-house with Uzziah, but to the devil,
that is the first step, and so to hell, without repentance. But if
their sin be not unpardonable, they may by repentance be
recovered, and in mercy tread these courts again. Now the way
to this recovery is to think seriously what they have done, or by
what way they went out from the house of God. Hence the
prophet is bid to show to the rebellious house, first the goings
out of the house, and then the comings in. But, I say, first he
bids show them the goings out thereof.[3] And this is of absolute
necessity for the recovering of the sinner. For until he that has
sinned himself out of God's house shall see what danger he has
incurred to himself by this his wicked going out, he will not
unfeignedly desire to come in thither again.

There is another thing as to this point to be taken notice of.
There is a way by which God also doth depart from this house,
and that also is by sin, as the occasion. The sin of a man will
thrust him out, and the sin of men will drive God out of his own
house. Of this you read, Ezekiel 11:22–23. For this, he saith, 'I
have forsaken mine house, I have left mine heritage, I have

---

[1] How careful ought churches to be in casting out an offending member,
seeing that their sentence should be as 'the judicial judgment of God.'
It is not revenge, hatred, malice, or the mere exercise of power, that is
to lead to it; it is *the good of the individual* that is to be pursued and
sought. While the church endeavours to remain pure, its aim and
object should be mainly to correct and reform the offender, that his
spirit may be saved. When discipline is undertaken from any other
motive than this; and when it is pursued from private pique, or
rivalship, or ambition, or the love of power, it is wrong. The salvation
of the offender, and the glory of God, should prompt to all the
measures which should be taken in the case. 'Restore such an one in
the spirit of meekness; considering thyself, lest thou also be tempted.'
Galatians 6:1.—(OFFOR.)

[2] Leviticus 20; 22:3; Ezekiel 14:8; 1 Corinthians 5:13.

[3] Ezekiel 43:10–11.

given the dearly beloved of my soul into the hand of her ene-mies.'[1] And this also is dreadful. The great sentence of Christ upon the Jews lay much in these words, 'Your house is left unto you desolate;' that is, God has left you to bare walls, and to lifeless traditions. Consider, therefore, of this going out also. Alas! a church, a true church, is but a poor thing if God leaves, if God forsakes it. By a true church I mean one that is congregated according to outward rule, that has sinned God away, as she had almost quite done that was of Laodicea.[2]

He that sins himself out, can find no good in the world; and they that have sinned God out, can find no good in the church. A church that has sinned God away from it, is a sad lump indeed. You therefore that are in God's church, take heed of sinning yourselves out thence; also take heed, that while you keep in, you sin not God away, for thenceforth no good is there. 'Yea, woe to them when I depart from them!' saith God.[3]

LIV. OF THE SINGERS BELONGING TO THE TEMPLE.

HAVING thus far passed through the temple, I now come to the singers there. The singers were many, but all of the church, either Jews or proselytes; nor was there any, as I know of, under the Old Testament worship, admitted to sing the songs of the church, and to celebrate that part of worship with the saints, but they who, at least in appearance, were so. The song of Moses, of Deborah, and of those that danced before David, with others that you read of, they were all performed, either by Jews by nature, or by such as were proselyted to their religion.[4] And such worship then was occasioned by God's great appearance for them, against the power of the Gentiles their enemies.

But we are confined to the songs of the temple, a more dis-tinct type of ours in the church under the gospel. 1. The singers then were many, but the chief of them, in the days of David, were David himself, Asaph, Jeduthun, and Heman, and their sons. 2. In David's time the chief of these singers were two hundred fourscore and eight.[5] These singers of old were to sing

---

[1] Jeremiah 12:7.

[2] Revelation 3.

[3] Hosea 9:12.

[4] Exodus 15:1; Jude 5:1–2; 1 Samuel 18:6.

[5] 1 Chronicles 25.

their songs over the burnt-offering, which were types of the
sacrificed body of Christ; a memorial of which offering we have
at the Lord's table, the consummation of which Christ and his
disciples celebrated with a hymn.[1] And as of old they were the
church that did sing in the temple, according to institution, to
God, so also they are by God's appointment to be sung in the
church by the new. Hence,

1. They are said to be the redeemed that sing. 2. The songs
that they sing are said to be the 'songs of their redemption.'[2] 3.
They were and are songs that no man can learn but they.

But let us run a little in the parallel.

1. They were of old appointed to sing, that were cunning and
skilful in songs. And answerable to that it is said, That no man
could learn our New Testament songs, but the hundred and
forty and four thousand which were redeemed from the earth.[3]

2. These songs were sung with harps, psalteries, cymbals,
and trumpets; a type of our singing with spiritual joy, from
grace in our hearts.[4]

3. The singers of old were to be clothed in fine linen; which
fine linen was a type of innocency, and an upright conversation.
Hence the singers under the New Testament are said to be
virgins, such in whose mouth was no guile, and that were
without 'fault before the throne of God.'[5]

4. The songs sung in the temple were new, or such as were
compiled after the manner of repeated mercies that the church
of God had received, or were to receive. And answerable to this,
is the church to sing now new songs, with new hearts, for new
mercies.[6] New songs, I say, are grounded on new matter, new
occasions, new mercies, new deliverances, new discoveries of
God to the soul, or for new frames of heart; and are such as are
most taking, most pleasing, and most refreshing to the soul.

5. These songs of old, to distinguish them from heathenish
ones, were called God's songs, the Lord's songs: because taught
by him, and learned of him, and enjoined to them, to be sung to

---

[1] Matthew 26:30.
[2] Revelation 5:9–10.
[3] 1 Chronicles 15:22; Revelation 14:3.
[4] 1 Chronicles 25:6; 2 Chronicles 29:26–28; Colossians 3:16.
[5] 1 Chronicles 15:27; Revelation 14:1–5; 7:9–16; Psalm 33:1.
[6] Psalm 33:3; 40:3; 96; 144:9; Revelation 14:3.

his praise. Hence David said, God had put a new song in his mouth, '*even* praise unto our God.'[1]

6. These songs also were called 'the songs of Zion,' and 'the songs of the temple.'[2] And they are so called as they were theirs to sing there; I say, of them of Zion, and the worshippers in the temple. I say, to sing in the church, by the church, to him who is the God of the church, for the mercies, benefits, and blessings which she has received from him. Sion-songs, temple-songs, must be sung by Sion's sons, and temple-worshippers.

The redeemed of the Lord shall return, and come to Zion with songs, and everlasting joy upon their heads, they shall obtain joy and gladness; and sorrow and sighing shall fly away. Therefore they shall come and sing in the height, or upon the mountain of Zion; and shall flow together thither, to the goodness of the Lord. 'Break forth into singing, ye mountains,' and let the inhabitants of the rock sing.[3]

To sing to God, is the highest worship we are capable of performing in heaven; and it is much if sinners on earth, without grace, should be capable of performing it, according to his institution, acceptably. I pray God it be done by all those that now-a-days get into churches, in spirit and with understanding.[4]

LV. OF THE UNION OF THE HOLY AND MOST HOLY TEMPLE.

THAT commonly called the temple of God at Jerusalem, considered as standing of two parts, was called the outward and inward temple, or, the holy and most holy place. They were built upon one and the same foundation; neither could one go into the holiest, but as through the holy place.[5]

The first house, namely, that which we have been speaking

---

[1] 1 Chronicles 25:7; Psalm 47:6–7; 137:4; 40:3.

[2] Psalm 137:3; Amos 8:3.

[3] Isaiah 44:23; 42:11; 51:11.

[4] In Bunyan's 'now a days,' it was much debated whether singing ought to be introduced in a mixed assembly. It was contended that a voice and talent for singing does not accompany the new birth; that it might tend to hypocrisy and vanity; and that it was not expressly commanded. The Quakers rejected it, but all other sects adopted that delightful part of public worship. See Keach's "Breach Repaired."—(OFFOR.)

[5] 1 Kings 3:1; 6:1; 2 Chronicles 5:1, 13; 7:2.

of, was a type of the church-militant, and the place most holy a type of the church-triumphant; I say, of the church-triumphant, as it now is.

So, then, the house standing of these two parts, was a shadow of the church both in heaven and earth. And for that they are joined together by one and the same foundation, it was to show, that they above, and we below, are yet one and the self-same house of God. Hence they, and we together, are called, 'The whole family in heaven and earth.'[1]

And hence it is said again, that we who believe on earth 'are come unto mount Zion, and unto the city of the living God, the heavenly Jerusalem, and to an innumerable company of angels, to the general assembly and church of the first-born, which are written in heaven, and to God the judge of all, and to the spirits of just men made perfect, and to Jesus the Mediator of the new covenant, and to the blood of sprinkling, that speaketh better things than *that of* Abel.'[2]

The difference, then, betwixt us and them is, not that we are really two, but one body in Christ, in divers places. True, we are below stairs, and they above; they in their holiday, and we in our working-day clothes; they in harbour, but we in the storm; they at rest, and we in the wilderness; they singing, as crowned with joy; we crying, as crowned with thorns. But, I say, we are all of one house, one family, and are all the children of one Father. This, therefore, we must not forget, lest we debar ourselves of much of that which otherwise, while here, we have a right unto. Let us, therefore, I say, remember, that the temple of God is but one, though divided, as one may say into kitchen and hall, above stairs and below; or holy and most holy place. For it stands upon the same foundation, and is called but one, the temple of God; which is built upon the Lord our Saviour.

I told you before, that none of old could go into the most holy, but by the holy place, even by the veil that made the partition between.[3] Wherefore, they are deceived that think to go into the holiest, which is heaven, when they die, who yet abandon and hate the holy place, while they live. Nay, Sirs, the way into the holiest is through the holy place; the way into heaven is through

---

[1] Ephesians 3:14–15.
[2] Hebrews 12:22–24.
[3] Exodus 26:33; Leviticus 16:2, 12, 15; Hebrews 9:7–8; 10:19.

the church on earth; for that Christ is there by his word to be received by faith, before he can by us in person be received in the beatical vision. The church on earth is as the house of the women, spoken of in the book of Esther, where we must be dieted, perfumed, and made fit to go into the bridegroom's chamber, or as Paul says, 'made meet to be partakers of the inheritance of the saints in light.'[1]

LVI. OF THE HOLIEST OR INNER TEMPLE.

THE most holy place was, as I said, a figure of heaven itself, consequently a type of that where the most special presence of God is, and where his face is most clearly seen, and the gladness of his countenance most enjoyed.[2]

The most holy place was dark, it had no windows in it, though there were such round the chambers; the more special presence of God, too, on Mount Sinai, was in the thick darkness there.[3]

1. This holiest, therefore, being thus made, was to show that God, as in heaven, to us on earth is altogether invisible, and not to be reached otherwise than by faith. For, I say, in that this house had no windows, nothing therein could be seen by the highest light of this world. Things there were only seen by the light of the fire of the altar, which was a type of the shinings of the Holy Ghost.[4] And hence it is said, notwithstanding this darkness, 'He dwelleth in the light, which no man can approach unto;' none but the high-priest, Christ.[5]

2. The holiest, therefore, was thus built, to show how different our state in heaven will be from this our state on earth. We walk here by one light, by the light of a written word; for that is now a light to our feet, and a lanthorn to our path. But that place, where there will be no written word, nor ordinances as here, will yet to us shine more light and clear, than if all the lights that are in the world were put together, to light one man. 'For God is light, and in him is no darkness at all.'[6] And in his

---

[1] Esther 2; Colossians 1:12.

[2] Hebrews 9:23–24; Exodus 25:22; Numbers 7:89.

[3] 1 Kings 8:12; 2 Chronicles 7:1; Exodus 19:9; 20:21.

[4] 1 Corinthians 2.

[5] 1 Timothy 6:16; 1 Peter 3:21–22.

[6] 1 John 1:5.

light, and in the light of the Lamb immediately, we shall live,
and walk, and rejoice all the days of eternity.

3. This also was ordained thus, to show that we, while in the
first temple, should live by faith, as to what there was, or as to
what was done in the second. Hence it is said, as to that, 'we walk
by faith, not by sight.'[1] The things that are there we are told of,
even of the ark of the testimony, and mercy-seat, and the cherubims of glory, and the presence of Christ, and of God: we are, I say,
told of them by the word, and believe, and are taken therewith,
and hope to go to them hereafter; but otherwise we see them not.
Therefore we are said to 'look, not at the things which are seen, but
at the things which are not seen; for the things which are seen *are*
temporal, but the things which are not seen *are* eternal.'[2]

4. The people of old were not to look into the holiest, lest they
died, save only their high-priest, he might go into it.[3] To show
that we, while here, must have a care of vain speculations, for
there is nothing to be seen, by us while here, in heaven, otherwise than by faith in God's eternal testament. True, we may
now come to the holiest, even as nigh as the first temple will
admit us to come; but it must be by blood and faith, not by vain
imagination, sense, or carnal reason.[4]

5. This holiest of all was four square every way, both as to
height, length, and breadth. To be thus, is a note of perfection,
as I have showed elsewhere; wherefore it was on purpose thus
built, to show us that all fulness of blessedness is there, both as
to the nature, degree, and duration. So 'when that which is
perfect is come, then that which is in part shall be done away.'[5]

LVII. OF THE VEIL OF THE TEMPLE.

THE veil of the temple was a hanging made of 'blue and purple,
and scarlet, and fine twined linen,' and there were cherubims
wrought thereon.[6]

1. This veil was one partition, betwixt the holy and most holy
place; and I take it, it was to keep from the sight of the worship-

---

[1] 2 Corinthians 5:9.
[2] 2 Corinthians 4:18.
[3] Numbers 17:13.
[4] Hebrews 10:19.
[5] 1 Corinthians 13:8–10; Hebrews 10:19–22.
[6] Exodus 26:31.

pers the things most holy, when the high-priest went in thither, to accomplish the service of God.[1]

2. The veil was a type of two things.

(1.) Of these visible heavens through which Christ passed when he went to make intercession for us. And as by the veil, the priest went out of the sight of the people, when he went into the holiest of all, so Jesus Christ when he ascended, was by the heavens, that great and stretched out curtain, received out of the sight of his people here. Also by the same curtain, since it is become as a tent for him to dwell in, he is still received, and still kept out of our sight; for now we see him not, nor shall, until these heavens be rolled together as a scroll, and pass away like a thing rolled together.[2]

(2.) This is that veil through which the apostle saith, Jesus is, as a forerunner for us, entered into the presence of God. For by veil here also must be meant the heavens, or outspread firmament thereof; as both Mark and Peter say, He 'is gone into heaven, and is on the right hand of God.'[3]

3. The veil of the temple was made of blue, the very colour of the heaven. Of purple and crimson, and scarlet also, which are the colours of many of the clouds, because of the reflections of the sun. But again,

4. The veil was also a type of the body of Christ. For as the veil of the temple, when whole, kept the view of the things of the holiest from us, but when rent, gave place to man to look in unto them; even so the body of Christ, while whole, kept the things of the holiest from that view, we, since he was pierced, have of them. Hence we are said to enter into the holiest, by faith, through the veil, that is to say, his flesh.[4] But yet, I say, all is by faith; and, indeed, the rending of the veil that day that Christ was crucified, did loudly preach this to us. For no sooner was the body of Christ pierced, but the veil of the temple rent in twain from the top to the bottom; and so a way was made for a clearer sight of what was there beyond it, both in the type and antitype.[5]

Thus you see that the veil of the temple was a type of these visible heavens, and also of the body of Christ; of the first,

---

[1] Exodus 26:33; 2 Chronicles 3:14; Hebrews 9:8.
[2] Isaiah 40:22; Acts 1:9–11; 3:19–21; 1 Peter 1:8.
[3] Mark 16:19; 1 Peter 3:22.
[4] Hebrews 10:19–22.
[5] Matthew 27:50–53; Hebrews 10:19–20.

because he passed through it unto the Father; of the second, because we by it have boldness to come to the Father.

I read also of two other veils, as of that spread over the face of Moses, to the end that the children of Israel should not stedfastly behold; and of the first veil of the tabernacle. But of these I shall not in this place speak.

Upon the veil of the temple there were also the figures of cherubims wrought, that is, of angels; to show, that as the angels are with us here, and wait upon us all the days of our pilgrimage in this world; so when we die, they stand ready, even at the veil, at the door of these heavens, to come when bid, to fetch us, and carry us away into Abraham's bosom.[1]

The veil, then, thus understood, teaches us first where Jesus is, namely, not here, but gone into heaven, from whence we should wait for him. It also teaches us, that if we would even now discern the glories that are in the holiest of all, we must look through Jesus to them, even through the veil, 'that is to say, his flesh.' Yea, it teaches us that we may, by faith through him, attain to a kind of a presence, at least of the beauty and sweetness of them.

LVIII. OF THE DOORS OF THE INNER TEMPLE.

1. Besides the veil, there was a door to the inner temple, and that door was made of olive-tree; 'and for the entering of the oracle, he made doors *of* olive-tree. The two doors also of olive-tree, and he carved upon them . . . cherubims, and palm trees, and open flowers, and overlaid *them* with gold, and spread gold upon the cherubims, and upon the palm trees.'[2]

2. These doors were a type of the gate of heaven, even of that which lets into the eternal mansion-house that is beyond that veil. I told you before that the veil was a type of the visible heavens, which God has spread out as a curtain, and through which Christ went when he ascended to the right hand of the Father.

3. Now, beyond this veil, as I said, I find a door, a gate opening with two leaves, as afore we found at the door of the outward temple. These are they which the Psalmist calls to, when he

---

[1] Luke 16:22.
[2] 1 Kings 6:31.

saith, 'Lift up your heads, O ye gates, even lift *them* up, ye everlasting doors, and the King of glory shall come in.'[1]

4. The doors of the temple were made of fir, but these, as you see, were made of olive: to show us by that fat tree, that rich type, with what glory we shall be met, who shall be counted worthy to enter at these gates. The olive tree has its name from the oil and fatness of its nature, and the doors that let into the holiest were made of this olive tree.[2,3]

5. Cherubims were also carved upon these doors to show, that as the angels met us at the temple door, and as they wait upon us in the temple, and stand also ready at the veil, so even at the gate of the mansion-house, they will be also ready to give us a welcome thither, and to attend us into the presence chamber.

6. Palm trees also, as they were carved upon the temple doors, so we also find them here before the oracle, upon the doors that let in thither; to show, that as Christ gave us the victory at our first entering into faith, so he will finish that victory, by giving of us eternal salvation. Thus is he the author and finisher of our faith. For as sure as at first we received the palm branch by faith, so surely shall we wear it in our hands, as a token of his faithfulness in the heaven of heavens, for ever.[4]

7. Open flowers are also carved here, to show that Christ, who is the door to glory, as well as the door to grace, will be precious to us at our entering in thither, as well as at the first step we took thitherward in a sinful and miserable world. Christ will never lose his sweet scent in the nostrils of his church. He is most sweet now, will be so at death, and sweetest of all, when by him we shall enter into that mansion-house prepared for us in heaven.

8. The palm trees and open flowers may also be a type of the precious ones of God, who shall be counted worthy of his kingdom; the one, of the uprightness of their hearts; the other, of the

---

[1] Psalm 24:7, 9.

[2] Romans 11:16–18.

[3] The olive wood is used, with, ivory and mother of pearl, in ornamenting the most sumptuous apartments in oriental palaces. It is exceedingly durable and elegant. 'The choosing olive out of every other kind of wood, for the adorning these sumptuous apartments, shows the elegance and grandeur of the taste in which Solomon's temple was built, where the doors of the oracle, and some other parts, were of olive wood.'—(Harmer, Schenzer, Lady M. W. Montague.)—(OFFOR.)

[4] Revelation 7:9.

good favour of their lives. 'The upright shall dwell in thy presence; and to him that ordereth his conversation aright, I will
show the salvation of God.'[1]

9. Thus sweet on earth, sweet in heaven; and he that yields
the fruit of the gospel here, shall find it for himself, and his
eternal comfort, at the gates of glory.

10. All these were overlaid with gold, as you may say, and so
they were at the door of the first house. True, but observe here
we have an addition. Here is gold upon gold. Gold laid on them,
and then gold spread upon that. He overlaid them with gold,
and then spread gold upon them. The Lord gives grace and
glory.[2] Gold and gold. Gold spread upon gold. Grace is gold in
the leaf, and glory is gold in plates. Grace is thin gold, glory is
gold that is thick. Here is gold laid on, and gold spread upon
that: and that both upon the palm trees and the cherubims.
Gold upon the palm trees, that is, on the saints; gold upon the
cherubims, that is, upon the angels. For I doubt not but that the
angels themselves shall receive additional glory for the service
which they have served Christ and his church on earth.

11. The angels are God's harvest men, and doubtless he will
give them good wages, even glory upon their glory then.[3]

12. You know harvest men use to be paid well for gathering
in the corn, and I doubt not but so shall these, when the great
ingathering is over. But what an entrance into life is here? Here
is gold upon gold at the door, at our first step into the kingdom.

LIX. OF THE GOLDEN NAILS OF THE INNER TEMPLE.

I SHALL not concern myself with all the nails of the temple, as of
those made of iron, etc.[4] But only with the golden ones, of which you
read, where he saith, 'And the weight of the nails *was* fifty shekels
of gold.'[5] These nails, as I conceive, were all fastened to the place
most holy, and of form most apt to that of which they were a figure.

1. Some of them represented Christ Jesus our Lord as fixed in
his mediatory office in the heavens; wherefore in one place,
when the Holy Ghost speaks of Christ, as he sprang from Judah

---

[1] Psalm 140:13.
[2] Psalm 84:11.
[3] Matthew 13:38–39; 24:31; John 4:36.
[4] 1 Chronicles 22:3.
[5] 2 Chronicles 3:9.

to be a mediator, saith, 'Out of him came the corner,' the corner
stone, 'out of him the nail.'[1] Now, since he is compared to a nail,
a golden nail, it is to show, that as a nail, by driving, is fixed in
his place; so Christ, by God's oath, is made an everlasting
priest.[2] Therefore, as he saith again, the nail, the Aaronical
priesthood, that was fastened in a sure place, should be removed, be cut down, and fall; so he who has the key of David,
which is Christ,[3] shall by God, as a nail, be fastened in a sure
place, and abide; therefore he says again, 'And he shall be for a
glorious throne,' or mercy-seat, 'to his Father's house.' And
moreover, That 'they shall hang upon him,' as on a nail, 'all the
glory of his Father's house, the offspring, and the issue, all
vessels of small quantity, from the vessels of cups, even to all
the vessels of flagons.'[4] According to that which is written, 'And
they sang a new song' to the Lamb that was slain, 'saying, Thou
art worthy,' etc.[5]

And therefore it is again that Christ, under the similitude of a
nail, is accounted by saints indeed their great pledge or hope, as
he is in heaven, of their certain coming thither. Hence they said
of old, God has given us 'a nail in his holy place;' a nail, says the
line, 'a pin, a constant and sure abode,' says the margin.[6] Now,
this nail in his holy place, as was showed before, is Christ; Christ,
as possessed of heaven, and as abiding, and ever living therein for
us. Hence he is called, as there, our head, our life, and our salvation; and also we are said there to be set down together in him.[7]

2. Some of these nails were types of the holy words of God,
which for ever are settled in heaven. Types, I say, of their 'yea
and amen.' Hence Solomon, in another place, compares the
words of the wise God, 'to goads and nails, fastened by the
masters of assemblies, *which* are given from one shepherd.'[8]

They are called goads, because, as such prick the oxen on in
their drawing, so God's words prick Christians on in their holy
duties. They are called nails, to show, that as nails, when

---

[1] Zechariah 10:4.
[2] Hebrews 7:25.
[3] Revelation 3:7.
[4] Isaiah 22:20–25.
[5] Revelation 5:9–12.
[6] Ezra 9:8.
[7] Ephesians 1; Colossians 3:3; Ephesians 2:5–6.
[8] Ecclesiastes 12:11.

fastened well in a sure place, are not easily removed; so God's words, by his will, stand firm for ever. The masters of the assemblies are first, the apostles. The one shepherd is Jesus Christ. Hence the gospel of Christ is said to be everlasting, to abide for ever, and to be more stedfast than heaven and earth.[1] The Lord Jesus then, and his holy words, are the golden nails of the temple, and the fixing of these nails in the temple, was to show that Christ is the same today, yesterday, and for ever; and that his words abide, and remain the same for ever and ever. He then that hath Christ, has a nail in the holiest; he that hath a promise of salvation hath also a nail in heaven, a golden nail in heaven!

LX. OF THE FLOOR AND WALLS OF THE INNER TEMPLE.

1. The floor of the oracle was overlaid with cedar, and so also were the walls of this house. 'He built twenty cubits on the sides of the house, both the floor and the walls with boards of cedar. He even built for it within, for the oracle, for the most holy *place*.'[2]

2. In that he doth tell us with what it was ceiled, and doth also thus repeat, saying, 'for the oracle, for it within, *even* for the most holy place,' it is because he would have it noted, that this only is the place that thus was done.

3. Twenty cubits, that was the length, and breadth, and height of the house; so that by his thus saying he teacheth that thus it was built round about.

4. The cedar is, if I mistake not, the highest of the trees.[3] Now in that it is said the house, the oracle, was ceiled round about therewith, it may be to show, that in heaven, and no where else, is the height of all perfections. Perfection is in the church on earth, but not such as is in heaven.

(1.) There is a natural perfection, and so a penny is as natural silver as is a shilling. (2.) There is a comparative perfection, and so one thing may be perfect and imperfect at the same time; as a half-crown is more than a shilling, yet less than a crown. (3.) There is also that which we call the utmost perfection, and that is it which cannot be added to, or taken from him; and so

---

[1] Isaiah 40:6–8; 1 Peter 1:24–25; Hebrews 13:20; Revelation 14:6; Matthew 24:35.

[2] 1 Kings 6:16.

[3] Ezekiel 31:3–8.

God only is perfect. Now, heavenly glory is that which goes beyond all perfection on the earth, as the cedar goes beyond all trees for height. Hence God, when he speaks of his own excellency, sets it forth by its height. The high God, the most High, and the high and lofty One; and the Highest.[1] These terms also are ascribed to this house, for that it was the place where utmost perfection dwelt.

I take, therefore, the cedar in this place to be a note of perfection, even the cedar with which this house was ceiled. For since it is the wisdom of God to speak to us ofttimes by trees, gold, silver, stones, beasts, fowls, fishes, spiders, ants, frogs, flies, lice, dust, etc., and here by wood; how should we by them understand his voice, if we count there is no meaning in them? 'And the cedar of the house within *was* carved with knops and open flowers; all *was* cedar; there was no stone seen.'[2]

Knops and flowers were they with which the golden candlestick was adorned, as you read, Exodus 25:33, 35; Exodus 37:10, 21. The candlestick was a type of the church, and the knops and flowers a type of her ornaments. But what! must heaven be hanged round about with the ornaments of saints! with the fruits of their graces! Well, it is certain that something more than ordinary must be done with them, since they are admitted to follow them into the holy place,[3] and since, it is said, they shall have 'a far more exceeding and eternal weight of glory bestowed on them, for them in the heavens.'[4]

'All *was* cedar; there was no stone seen.' Take stone in the type for that which was really so, and in the antitype for that which is so mystically, and then it may import to us, that in heaven, the antitype of this holiest, there shall never be anything of hardness of heart in them that possess it for ever. All imperfection ariseth from the badness of the heart, but there will be no bad hearts in glory. No shortness in knowledge, no crossness of disposition, no workings of lusts, or corruptions will be there; no, not throughout the whole heavens. Here, alas! they are seen, and that in the best of saints, because here our light is mixed with darkness; but there will be no night there, nor any stone seen.

---

[1] Psalm 97:9; 138:6; Genesis 14:19–21; Daniel 3:26; 5:18; Psalm 18:13; 87:5; Luke 1:32; 6:35; Isaiah 57:15; Psalm 9:2; 56:2; 92:1; Isaiah 14:14.
[2] 1 Kings 6:18.
[3] Revelation 14:13.
[4] 2 Corinthians 4:16–17.

'And the floor of the house was overlaid with gold.'[1] This is like that of which we read of the New Jerusalem that is to come from God out of heaven; says the text, 'The street of the city was pure gold;' and like that of which you read in Exodus, 'They saw the God of Israel, and under his feet as it were a paved work of a sapphire stone, and as it were the body of heaven in *his* clearness.'[2] All the visions were rich, but this the richest, that the floor of the house should be covered or overlaid with gold. The floor and street are walking-places, and how rich will our steps be then! Alas! here we sometimes fall into the mire, and then again stumble upon blocks and stones. Here we sometimes fall into holes, and have our heel oft catched in a snare; but there will be none of these. Gold! gold! all will be gold, and golden perfections, when we come into the holy place! Job at best took but his steps in butter, but we then shall take all our steps in the gold of the sanctuary.

LXI. OF THE ARK OF THE COVENANT WHICH WAS PLACED IN THE INNER TEMPLE.

IN the Word I read of three arks; to wit, Noah's ark, that in which Moses was hid, and the ark of the covenant of God.[3] But it is the ark of the covenant of which I shall now speak. The ark was made 'of shittim-wood, two cubits and a half *was the* length thereof, and a cubit and a half the breadth thereof, and a cubit and a half the height thereof.' It was overlaid 'with pure gold within and without,' and 'a crown of gold' was made for it 'round about.'[4]

1. This ark was called 'the ark of the covenant,' as the first that you read of was called 'Noah's,' because as he in that was kept from being drowned, so the tables of the covenant were kept in this from breaking.

2. This ark, in this, was a type of Christ; for that in him only, and not in the hand of Moses, these tables were kept whole. Moses brake them, the ark keeps them.

3. Not only that wrote on two tables of stone, but that also called 'the ceremonial,' was put into the ark to be kept. The two tables were put into the midst of the ark, to answer to this— thy law is within my heart to do it. But the ceremonial was put

---

[1] 1 Kings 6:30.
[2] Revelation 21:21; Exodus 24:10.
[3] Genesis 6:14; Exodus 2:3, 5.
[4] Exodus 25:10–11.

into the side of the ark, to show that out of the side of Christ must come that which must answer that, for out thence came blood and water; blood, to answer the blood of the ceremonies; and water, to answer the purifyings and rinsings of that law. The ceremonies, therefore, were lodged in the side of the ark, to show that they should be answered out of the side of Jesus Christ.[1]

4. The ark had the name of God put upon it; yea, it was called the strength of God, and his glory, though made of wood. And Christ is God both in name and nature, though made flesh; yea more, made to be sin for us.[2]

5. The ark was carried upon men's shoulders this way and that, to show how Christ should be carried and preached by his apostles and ministers into all parts of the world.[3]

6. The ark had those testimonies of God's presence accompanying it, as had no other ceremony of the law; and Christ had those signs and tokens of his presence with him, as never had man either in law or gospel. This is so apparent it needs no proof. And now for a few comparisons more.

(1.) It was at that that God answered the people, when they were wont to come to inquire of him; and in these last days God has spoken to us by his Son.[4]

(2.) At the presence of the ark the waters of Jordan stood still till Israel, the ransomed of the Lord, passed over from the wilderness to Canaan; and it is by the power and presence of Christ that we pass over death, Jordan's antitype, from the wilderness of this world to heaven.[5]

(3.) Before the ark the walls of Jericho fell down; and at the presence of Christ shall all high towers, and strongholds, and hiding places for sinners be razed, and dissolved at his coming.[6]

(4.) Before the ark Dagon fell, that idol of the Philistines; and before Christ Jesus devils fell, those gods of all those idols. And

---

[1] Exodus 25:16–17; Deuteronomy 10:5; Psalm 40:8; John 19:34; Hebrews 10:7.

[2] 2 Samuel 6:2; 1 Chronicles 13:6; 2 Chronicles 6:1; John 1:14; Romans 9:5; 2 Corinthians 5:21.

[3] Exodus 25:14; 1 Chronicles 15:15; Matthew 28:19–20; Luke 24:46–47.

[4] 1 Chronicles 13:3; 1 Samuel 14:18; Hebrews 1:2; John 16:23–24.

[5] Joshua 3:15–17; John 11:25; Romans 8:37–39; 1 Corinthians 15:54–57.

[6] Joshua 6:20; Isaiah 30:25; 2:10, 16; 2 Peter 3:10; Revelation 20:11–13.

he must reign till all his enemies be put under his feet, and until they be made his footstool.[1]

(5.) The Philistines were also plagued for meddling with the ark, while they abode uncircumcised; and the wicked will one day be most severely plagued for their meddling with Christ, with their uncircumcised hearts.[2]

(6.) God's blessing was upon those that entertained the ark as they should; and much more is, and will his blessing be upon those that so embrace and entertain his Christ, and profess his name sincerely.[3]

(7.) When Uzzah put forth his hand to stay the ark, when the oxen shook it, as despairing of God's protecting of it without a human help, he died before the Lord; even so will all those do, without repentance, who use unlawful means to promote Christ's religion, and to support it in the world.[4]

(8.) The ark, though thus dignified, was of itself but low—but a cubit and a half high; also Christ—though he was the glory of heaven and of God—yet made himself of no reputation, and was found in the likeness of a man.[5]

(9.) The ark had a crown of gold round about upon it, to show how Christ is crowned by his saints by faith, and shall be crowned by them in glory, for all the good he hath done for them; as also how all crowns shall one day stoop to him, and be set upon his head. This is showed in the type.[6] And in the antitype.[7]

(10.) The ark was overlaid with gold within and without, to show that Christ was perfect in inward grace and outward life, in spirit and in righteousness.[8]

(11.) The ark was placed under the mercy-seat, to show that Jesus Christ, as Redeemer, brings and bears, as it were, upon

---

[1] 1 Samuel 5:1–4; Mark 5:12; 1 Corinthians 15:25; Hebrews 10:13.
[2] 1 Samuel 5:6–13; Psalm 50:6; Matthew 24:51; 25:11–12;
   Luke 13:25–29.
[3] 2 Samuel 6:11; Acts 3:26; Galatians 3:13–14; Matthew 19:27–29;
   Luke 22:28–29.
[4] 1 Chronicles 13:9–10; Matthew 26:52; Revelation 13:10.
[5] Exodus 25:10–12; Philippians 2:6–11.
[6] Zechariah 6:11, 14.
[7] Revelation 4:10; 19:12.
[8] John 1:14; 1 Peter 2:22.

his shoulders, the mercy of God to us, even in the body of his flesh, through death.[1]

(12.) When the ark was removed far from the people, the godly went mourning after it; and when Christ is hid, or taken from us, then we mourn in those days.[2]

(13.) All Israel had the ark again, after their mourning-time was over; and Christ, after his people have sorrowed for him a while, will see them again, 'and their hearts shall rejoice.'[3]

By all these things, and many more that might be mentioned, it is most evident that the ark of the testimony was a type of Jesus Christ; and take notice a little of that which follows, namely, that the ark at last arrived to the place most holy.[4] That is, after its wanderings; for the ark was first made to wander, like a non-inhabitant, from place to place; now hither, and then thither; now in the hands of enemies, and then abused by friends; yea, it was caused to rove from place to place, as that of which the world was weary. I need instance to you for proof hereof none other place than the fifth, sixth, and seventh chapters of the first Book of Samuel; and, answerable to this, was our dear Lord Jesus posted backwards and forwards, hither and thither, by the force of the rage of his enemies. He was hunted into Egypt so soon as he was born.[5] Then he was driven to live in Galilee the space of many years. Also, when he showed himself to Israel, they drove him sometimes into the wilderness, sometimes into the desert, sometimes into the sea, and sometimes into the mountains, and still in every of these places he was either haunted or hunted by new enemies.

And at last of all, the Pharisees plot for his life; Judas sells him, the priests buy him, Peter denies him, his enemies mock, scourge, buffet, and much abuse him. In fine, they get him condemned, and crucified, and buried; but at last God commanded, and took him to his place, even within the veil, and sets him to bear up the mercy-seat, where he is to this very day, being our ark to save us, as Noah's did him, as Moses' did him; yea, better, as none but Christ doth save his own.

---

[1] Exodus 25:21; Ephesians 4:22; 5:1–2.
[2] 2 Samuel 7:2; Mark 2:19–20; Luke 5:34–35; John 16:20–22.
[3] John 16:1–3, 20–22.
[4] Hebrews 9:3–4.
[5] Matthew 2.

LXII. OF THE PLACING OF THE ARK
IN THE HOLIEST, OR INNER TEMPLE.

1. The ark, as we have said, and as the text declares, when carried to its rest, was placed in the inner temple, or in the most holy place, '*even* under the wings of the cherubims.' 'And the priests brought in the ark of the covenant of the Lord unto his place, to the oracle of the house, into the most holy *place, even* under the wings of the cherubims.'[1]

2. Before this, as was said afore, the ark was carried from place to place, and caused to dwell in a tent under curtains, as all our fathers did; to show that Christ, as we, was made for a time to wander in the world, in order to his being possessed of glory.[2]

3. But now, when the ark was brought into the holiest, it is said to be brought into its place. This world then was not Christ's place, he was not from beneath, he came from his Father's house; wherefore while here, he was not at his place, nor could until he ascended up where he was before.[3]

4. Christ's proper place, therefore, is the holiest. His proper place, as God, as Priest, as Prophet, as King, and as the Advocate of his people. Here, with us, he has no more to do, in person, as mediator. If he were on earth, he should not be a priest, etc. His place and work is now above with his Father, and before the angels.[4]

5. It is said the ark was brought 'to the oracle of the house,' Solomon was not content to say it was brought into the holiest; but he saith, his place was the oracle, the holy oracle, that is, the place of hearing. For he, when he ascended, had somewhat to say to God on the behalf of his people. To the oracle, that is, to the place of revealing. For he also was there to receive, and from thence to reveal to his church on earth, something that could not be made manifest but from this holy oracle. There therefore he is with the two tables of testimony in his heart, as perfectly kept; he also is there with the whole fulfilling of the ceremonial law in his side, showing and pleading the perfection of his

---

[1] Exodus 26:33; 39:35; 1 Kings 8:3; 2 Chronicles 5:7.

[2] 2 Samuel 7:1, 3, 6; Hebrews 11:9; John 1:10; 16:28; 3:13.

[3] John 8:23; 16:28; 6:62; 3:13.

[4] Acts 5:31; 1 Peter 3:22; Hebrews 4:14; 8:4; 9:24;1 John 2:1–2; Revelation 1:4–5.

righteousness, and the merit of his blood with his Father, and to receive and to do us good, who believe in him, how well pleased the Father is with what he has done in our behalf.

6. 'Into the most holy place.' By these words is showed, whither also the ark went, when it went to take up its rest. And in that this ark was a type of Christ in this, it is to show or further manifest, that what Christ doth now in heaven, he doth it before his Father's face. Yea, it intimates, that Christ even there makes his appeals to God, concerning the worth of what he did on earth; to God the Judge of all, I say, whether he ought not for his suffering-sake to have granted to him his whole desire, as Priest and Advocate for his people?

'Wilt thou,' said Festus to Paul, 'go up to Jerusalem, and there be judged of these things before me?'[1] Why, this our blessed Jesus was willing, when here, to go up to Jerusalem to be judged; and being misjudged of there, he made his appeal to God, and is now gone thither, even into the holy place, even to him that is Judge of all, for his verdict upon his doing; and whether the souls for whom he became undertaker, to bring them to glory, have not by him a right to the kingdom of heaven.

7. 'Under the wings of the cherubims.' This doth further confirm our words; for having appealed from earth to heaven, as the ark was set under the wings of the cherubims, so he, in his interceding with God and pleading his merits for us, doth it in the presence and hearing of all the angels in heaven.

And thus much of the ark of the covenant, and of its antitype. We come next to speak of the mercy-seat.

LXIII. OF THE MERCY-SEAT, AND HOW IT WAS PLACED IN THE HOLY TEMPLE.

THE mercy-seat was made in the wilderness, but brought up by Solomon, after the temple was built, with the rest of the holy things.[2]

The mercy-seat, as I have showed of the ark, was but low. 'Two cubits and a half was the length, and a cubit and a half the breadth thereof;' but the height thereof 'was without measure.'

1. The length and breadth of the mercy-seat is the same with

---

[1] Acts 25:9.
[2] 2 Chronicles 5:2–10.

that of the ark: perhaps to show us, that the length and breadth
of the mercy of God to his elect, is the same with the length and
breadth of the merits of Christ.[1] Therefore, we are said to be
justified in him, blessed in him, even according to the purpose
which God purposed in him.

2. But in that the mercy-seat is without measure, as to
height, it is to show, that would God extend it, it is able to reach
even them that fall from heaven, and to save all that ever lived
on earth, even all that are now in hell. For there is not only
breadth enough for them that shall be saved, but 'bread enough
and to spare.'[2] 'And thou shalt,' says God, 'put the mercy-seat
above upon the ark.' Thus he said to Moses, and this was the
place which David assigned for it.[3] Now, its being by God's
ordinance placed thus, doth teach us many things.

(1.) That mercy's foundation to us is Christ. The mercy-seat
was set upon the ark of the testimony, and there it rested to
usward. Justice would not, could not have suffered us to have
had any benefit by mercy, had it not found an ark, a Christ to
rest upon. 'Deliver him,' saith God, 'from going down to the pit, I
have found a ransom.'[4]

(2.) In that it was placed above, it doth show also that Christ
was, of mercies, ordaining a fruit of mercy. Mercy is above, is
the ordainer; God is love, and sent of love his Son to be the
Saviour and propitiation for our sins.[5]

(3.) In that the mercy-seat and ark were thus joined together, it also shows, that without Christ mercy doth not act.
Hence, when the priest came of old to God for mercy, he did use
to come into the holy place with blood; yea, and did use to
sprinkle it upon the mercy-seat, and before it, seven times.
Take away the ark, and the mercy-seat will fall, or come
greatly down at least. So take away Christ, and the flood-gate
of mercy is let down, and the current of mercy stopped. This is
true, for so soon as Christ shall leave off to mediate, will come
the eternal judgment.

(4.) Again, in that the mercy-seat was set above upon the ark, it

---

[1] Exodus 25:10, 17.
[2] Luke 15:17.
[3] Exodus 25:21; 1 Chronicles 28:11.
[4] Job 33:24.
[5] John 3:16; 1 John 4:10.

teacheth us to know, that mercy can look down from heaven, though the law stand by and looks on; but then it must be in Christ, as kept there, and fulfilled by him for us. The law out of Christ is terrible as a lion; the law in him is meek as a lamb. The reason is, for that it finds in him enough to answer for all their faults, that come to God for mercy by him. 'Christ is the end of the law for righteousness;' and if that be true, the law for that can look no further upon whoever comes to God by him. The law did use to sentence terribly, until it was put into the ark to be kept.[1] But after it was said, 'It is there to be kept,' we read not of it as afore.[2]

(5.) Let them then that come to God for mercy be sure to come to him by the ark, Christ. For grace, as it descends to us from above the mercy-seat, so that mercy-seat doth rest upon the ark. Wherefore, sinner, come thou for mercy that way: for there if thou meetest with the law, it can do thee no harm; nor can mercy, shouldst thou elsewhere meet it, do thee good. Come, therefore, and come boldly to the throne of grace, this mercy-seat, thus borne up by the ark, and 'obtain mercy, and find grace to help in time of need.'[3]

Wherefore the thus placing of things in the holiest, is admirable to behold in the word of God. For that indeed is the glass by and through which we must behold this glory of the Lord. Here we see the reason of things; here we see how a just God can have to do, and that in a way of mercy, with one that has sinned against him. It is because the law has been kept by the Lord Jesus Christ; for as you see, the mercy-seat stands upon the ark of the covenant, and there God acts in a way of grace towards us.[4]

LXIV. OF THE LIVING WATERS OF THE INNER TEMPLE.

ALTHOUGH in the holy relation of the building of the temple no mention is made of these waters, but only of the mount on which, and the materials with which the king did build it, yet it seems to me that in that mount, and there too where the temple was built, there was a spring of living water. This seems more than probable, by Ezekiel 47:1, where he saith, 'He brought me again unto the

---

[1] As the mercy-seat covered the law deposited in the ark, so Christ covers the transgressions of his people; while Christ sits upon the mercy-seat, the law cannot rise up in judgment against them.—(Jennings.)

[2] 1 Kings 8:9; 2 Chronicles 5:10; Romans 10:4.

[3] Hebrews 4:16.

[4] Exodus 25:17–23.

door of the house, and behold, waters issued out from under the
threshold of the house eastward, for the fore-front of the house
stood toward the east, and the waters came down from under, from
the right side of the house, at the south *side* of the altar.' So again,
'And a fountain shall come forth of the house of the Lord, and shall
water the valley of Shittim.'[1] Nor was the spring, wherever was the
first appearance of these holy waters, but in the sanctuary, which
is the holiest of all,[2] where the mercy-seat stood, which in Revelations is called 'The throne of God, and of the Lamb.'[3]

This also is that which the prophet Zechariah means, when
he says, 'Living waters shall go out from Jerusalem, half of them
toward the former sea, and half of them toward the hinder sea,'
etc.[4] They are said to go forth from Jerusalem, because they
came down to the city from out of the sanctuary which stood in
Jerusalem. This is that which in another place is called a river
of water of life, because it comes forth from the throne, and
because it was at the head of it, as I suppose, used in and about
temple-worship. It was with this, I think, that the molten sea
and the ten lavers were filled, and in which the priests washed
their hands and feet when they went into the temple to do
service; and that also in which they washed the sacrifices before
they offered them to God; yea, I presume, all the washings and
rinsings about their worship was with this water.

This water is said in Ezekiel and Revelations to have the tree
of life grow on the banks of it, and was a type of the word and
Spirit of God, by which, both Christ himself sanctified himself,
in order to his worship as high-priest.[5] And also this water is
that which heals all those that shall be saved; and by which,
they being sanctified thereby also, do all their works of worship
and service acceptably, through Jesus Christ our Lord. This
water therefore is said to go forth into the sea, the world, and to
heal its fish, the sinners therein; yea, this is that water of which
Christ Jesus our Lord saith, Whosoever shall drink thereof shall
live for ever.[6]

---

[1] Joel 3:18.
[2] Ezekiel 47:12.
[3] Revelation 22:1–2.
[4] Zechariah 14:8.
[5] Ezekiel 47; Revelation 22.
[6] Ezekiel 47:8–10; Zechariah 14:8; John 4:14.

LXV. OF THE CHAINS WHICH WERE IN THE ORACLE OR INNER TEMPLE.

As there were chains on the pillars that stood before the porch of the temple, and in the first house; so, like unto them, there were chains in the holiest, here called the oracle. These chains were not chains in show, or as carved on wood, etc., but chains indeed, and that of gold; and they were prepared to make a partition 'before the oracle' within.[1]

I told you before that the holiest was called the oracle, not because in a strict sense the whole of it was so, but because such answer of God was there, as was not in the outward temple; but I think that the ark and mercy-seat were indeed more especially that called the oracle; 'for there I will meet with thee,' saith God, and from above that 'I will commune with thee.'[2] When David said, 'I lift up my hands toward thy holy oracle,' he meant not so much towards the holiest house, as toward the mercy-seat that was therein. Or, as he saith in the margin, 'Toward the oracle of thy sanctuary.'[3]

When therefore he saith, 'before the oracle,' he means, these chains were put in the most holy place, before the ark and mercy-seat, to give to Aaron and his sons to understand that an additional glory was there. For the ark and mercy-seat were preferred before that holy house itself, even as Christ and the grace of God is preferred before the highest heavens. 'The Lord *is* high above all nations, *and* his glory above the heavens.'[4]

So then, the partition that was made in this house by these chains, these golden chains, was not so much to divide the holy from the place most holy, as to show that there is in the holiest house that which is yet more worthy than it.

The holiest was a type of heaven, but the ark and mercy-seat were a type of Christ, and of the mercy of God to us by him; and I trow any man will conclude, if he knows what he says, that the God and Christ of heaven are more excellent than the house they dwell in. Hence David said again, 'Whom have I in heaven *but thee?*' For thou art more excellent than they.[5] For though

---

[1] 1 Kings 6:21; 2 Chronicles 3:16.
[2] Exodus 25:22.
[3] Psalm 28:2.
[4] Psalm 113:4.
[5] Psalm 73:25.

that which is called heaven would serve some; yea, though God himself was out of it, yet none but the God of heaven will satisfy a truly gracious man: it is God that the soul of this man thirsteth for; it is God that is his exceeding joy.[1]

These chains then, as they made this partition in the most holy place, may teach us, that when we shall be glorified in heaven, we shall yet, even then, and there, know that there will continue an infinite disproportion between God and us. The golden chains that are there will then distinguish [or separate] the Creator from the creature. For we, even we which shall be saved, shall yet retain our own nature, and shall still continue finite beings; yea, and shall there also see a disproportion between our Lord, our head, and us; for though now we are, and also then shall be like him as to his manhood; yea, and shall be like him also, as being glorified with his glory; yet he shall transcend and go beyond us, as to degree and splendour, as far as ever the highest king on earth did shine above the meanest subject that dwelt in his kingdom.

Chains have of old been made use of as notes of distinction, to show us who are bond men, and who free. Yea, they shall at the day of judgment be a note of distinction of bad and good; even as here they will distinguish the heavens from God, and the creature from the Creator.[2]

True, they are chains of sin and wrath, but these chains of gold; yet these chains, even these also will keep creatures in their place, that the Creator may have his glory, and receive those acknowledgments there from them, which is due unto his Majesty.[3]

LXVI. OF THE HIGH-PRIEST, AND OF HIS OFFICE IN THE INNER TEMPLE.

WHEN things were thus ordained in the house 'most holy,' then went the high-priest in thither, according as he was appointed, to do his office, which was to burn incense in his golden censer, and to sprinkle with his finger the blood of his sacrifice, for the people, upon and above the mercy-seat.[4]

Now for this special work of his, he had peculiar preparations.

---

[1] Psalm 42:2; 63:1; 143:6; 17:15; 43:4.
[2] 2 Peter 2:4; Jude 6; Matthew 22:13.
[3] Revelation 4; 5:11–14.
[4] Exodus 30:7–10; Leviticus 16:11–14.

1. He was to be washed in water. 2. Then he was to put on his holy garments. 3. After that he was to be anointed with holy oil. 4. Then an offering was to be offered for him, for the further fitting of him for his office. 5. The blood of this sacrifice must be put, some of it upon his right ear, some on the thumb of his right hand, and some on the great toe of his right foot. This done, some more of the blood, with the anointing oil, must be sprinkled upon him, and upon his garment; for after this man‐ner must he be consecrated to his work as high-priest.[1]

His being washed in water was to show the purity of Christ's humanity. His curious robes were a type of all the perfections of Christ's righteousness. The holy oil that was poured on his head was to show how Christ was anointed with the Holy Ghost unto his work, as priest. The sacrifice of his consecration was a type of that offering Christ offered in the garden when he mixed his sweat with his own blood, and tears, and cries, when he prayed to him that was able to save him; 'and was heard in that he feared;' for with his blood, as was Aaron with the blood of the bullock that was slain for him, was this blessed one besmeared from head to foot, when his sweat, as great drops or clodders of blood, fell down from head and face, and whole body, to the ground.[2]

When Aaron was thus prepared, then he offered his offering for the people, and carried the blood within the veil.[3] The which Christ Jesus also answered, when he offered his own body without the gate, and then carried his blood into the heavens, and sprinkled it before the mercy-seat.[4] For Aaron was a type of Christ; his offering, a type of Christ's offering his body; the blood of the sacrifice, a type of the blood of Christ; his garments, a type of Christ's righteousness; the mercy-seat, a type of the throne of grace; the incense, a type of Christ's praise; and the sprinkling of the blood of the sacrifice upon the mercy-seat, a type of Christ's pleading the virtue of his sufferings for us in the presence of God in heaven.[5]

'Wherefore, holy brethren, partakers of the heavenly calling,

---

[1] Exodus 29.
[2] Luke 22:44; Hebrews 10:20.
[3] Leviticus 16.
[4] Hebrews 13:11–12; 9:11–12, 24.
[5] Hebrews 9:10–28.

consider the apostle and high priest of our profession, Christ Jesus.'[1] 'Seeing then that we have a great high priest, that is passed into the heavens, Jesus the Son of God, let us hold fast *our* profession. For we have not an high priest which cannot be touched with the feeling of our infirmities; but was in all points tempted like as *we are, yet* without sin. Let us therefore come boldly unto the throne of grace, that we may obtain mercy, and find grace to help in time of need. For every high priest taken from among men is ordained for men in things *pertaining* to God, that he may offer both gifts and sacrifices for sins: who can have compassion on the ignorant, and on them that are out of the way; for that he himself also is compassed with infirmity.'[2]

This then is our high priest; and this was made so 'not after the law of a carnal commandment, but after the power of an endless life.' For Aaron and his sons were made priests without an oath, 'but this with an oath by him that said unto him, The Lord sware and will not repent, Thou *art* a priest for ever after the order of Melchisedec. By so much was Jesus made a surety of a better testament.'

'And they truly were many priests, because they were not suffered to continue by reason of death. But this *man*, because he continueth ever, hath an unchangeable priesthood. Wherefore he is able also to save them to the uttermost that come unto God by him, seeing he ever liveth to make intercession for them. For such an high priest became us, *who is* holy, harmless, undefiled, separate from sinners, and made higher than the heavens; who needeth not daily, as those high priests, to offer up sacrifice, first for his own sins, and then for the people's: for this he did once, when he offered up himself. For the law maketh men high priests which have infirmity; but the word of the oath, which was since the law, *maketh* the Son, who is consecrated for evermore. Now of the things which we have spoken *this is* the sum: We have such an high priest, who is set on the right hand of the throne of the majesty in the heavens; a minister of the sanctuary, and of the true tabernacle,[3] which the Lord pitched, and not man. For every high priest is ordained to offer gifts and sacrifices:

---

[1] Hebrews 3:1.

[2] Hebrews 4:14–16; 5:1–2.

[3] In Bunyan's edition this is called the 'new tabernacle,' a typographical error which is corrected by restoring the true reading.—(OFFOR.)

wherefore it is of necessity that this man have somewhat also to offer. For if he were on earth, he should not be a priest, seeing that there are priests that offer gifts according to the law: who serve unto the example and shadow of heavenly things, as Moses was admonished of God when he was about to make the tabernacle: for, See, saith he, *that* thou make all things according to the pattern showed to thee in the mount.'[1]

'But Christ being come an high priest of good things to come, by a greater and more perfect tabernacle, not made with hands, that is to say, not of this building; neither by the blood of goats and calves, but by his own blood, he entered in once into the holy place, having obtained eternal redemption *for us*. For if the blood of bulls and of goats, and the ashes of an heifer sprinkling the unclean, sanctifieth to the purifying of the flesh: how much more shall the blood of Christ, who through the eternal Spirit offered himself without spot to God, purge your conscience from dead works to serve the living God.

'For Christ is not entered into the holy places made with hands, which are the figures of the true; but into heaven itself, now to appear in the presence of God for us: Nor yet that he should offer himself often, as the high priest entereth into the holy place every year with blood of others; for then must he often have suffered since the foundation of the world: but now once in the end of the world hath he appeared to put away sin by the sacrifice of himself. And as it is appointed unto men once to die, but after this the judgment: so Christ was once offered to bear the sins of many; and unto them that look for him shall he appear the second time without sin unto salvation.'[2]

LXVII. OF THE HIGH-PRIEST'S GOING INTO THE HOLIEST ALONE.

As it was the privilege of the high-priest to go into the holiest alone, so there was something of mystery also, to which I shall speak a little: 'There shall,' says God, 'be no man in the tabernacle of the congregation, when he [Aaron] goeth in to make an atonement in the holy *place*, until he come out, and have made an atonement for himself, and for his household, and for all the

---

[1] Hebrews 7:16–8:5.
[2] Hebrews 9:11–14, 24–28.

congregation of Israel.'[1] The reason is, for that Christ is mediator alone; he trod the winepress alone; and of the people there
was none with him to help him there.[2]

Of the people there was none to help him to bear his cross, or
in the management of the first part of his priestly office. Why
then should there be any to share with him in his executing of
the second part thereof? Besides, he that helps an intercessor
must himself be innocent, or in favour, upon some grounds not
depending on the worth of the intercession. But as to the intercession of Christ, who can come in to help upon the account of
such innocency or worth? Not the highest angel; for there is
none such but one, wherefore he must do that alone. Hence it is
said, He went in alone, is there alone, and there intercedes
alone. And this is manifest not only in the type Aaron, but in the
antitype Christ Jesus.[3]

I do not say that there is no man in heaven but Jesus Christ;
but I say, he is there to make intercession for us alone. Yea, the
holy text says more. 'I go,' saith Christ, 'to prepare a place for you;
and if I go and prepare a place for you, I will come again and
receive you unto myself, that where I am *there ye* may be also.'[4]

This text seems to insinuate that Christ is in the holiest or
highest heavens alone; and that he there alone must be, until he
has finished his work of intercession; for not till then he comes
again to take us to himself. Let us grant Christ the pre-eminency
in this, as also in all other things; for he is intercessor for his
church, and makes it for them in the holiest alone. It is said he
is the light that no man can approach unto.

LXVIII. OF THE HIGH-PRIEST'S GOING
IN THITHER BUT ONCE A YEAR.

As the high-priest went into the holiest when he went in thither
alone; so to do that work, he went in thither but once a year.
Thou shalt not come 'at all times,' said God to him, 'into the holy
place, within the veil, before the mercy-seat, which *is* upon the
ark, that thou die not.'[5]

---

[1] Leviticus 16:17.
[2] Isaiah 63:3; 1 Timothy 2:5.
[3] Hebrews 6:19–20; 9:7–11, 21, 23–24.
[4] John 14:1–3.
[5] Leviticus 16:2.

And as he was to go in thither but 'once a year,' so not then neither, unless clothed and adorned, with his Aaronical holy robes.[1] Then he was to be clothed, as I hinted before, with the holy robes, the frontlet of gold upon his forehead, the names of the twelve tribes upon his breast, and the jingling bells upon the skirts of his garment? nor would all this do, unless he went in thither with blood.[2]

Now, this once a year the apostle taketh special notice of, and makes great use of it. 'Once a year,' saith he, this high-priest went in thither: once a year, that is, to show, that Christ should once in the end of the world, go into heaven itself, to make intercession there for us. For by this word 'year,' he shows the term and time of the world is meant; and by 'once' in that year, he means once in the end of the world.

'Not,' saith he, 'that he should offer himself often: as the high-priest entereth into the holy place every year with blood of others. For then must he often have suffered since the founda-tion of the world: but now once in the end of the world hath he appeared to put away sin by the sacrifice of himself.'[3]

And having thus once offered his sacrifice without the veil, he is now gone into the holiest, to perfect his work of mediation for us. Not into the holy places made with hands, which are the figures of the true, but into heaven itself, now to appear in the presence of God for us.

Now if our Lord Jesus is gone indeed, now to appear in the presence of God for us; and if this now be the once a year that the type speaks of; the once in the end of the world, as our apostle says; then it follows, that the people of God should all stand waiting for his benediction that to them he shall bring with him when he shall return from thence. Wherefore he adds, 'Christ was once offered to bear the sins of many; and unto them that look for him shall he appear the second time without sin unto salvation.'[4]

This, therefore, shows us the greatness of the work that Christ has to do at the right hand of God, for that he stays there so long. He accomplished all the first part of his priesthood in less than forty years, if you take in the making of his holy garments and all; but about this second part thereof, he has been above in

---

[1] Leviticus 16:32–34.

[2] Exodus 28; Leviticus 16.

[3] Hebrews 9:25–26.

[4] Hebrews 9:28.

heaven above sixteen hundred years, and yet has not done.

This therefore calls for faith and patience in saints, and by this he also tries the world; so that they, in mocking manner, begin to say already, 'Where is the promise of his coming?'[1] But I say again, We must look and wait. If the people waited for Zacharias, and wondered that he staid so long, because he staid in the holy place somewhat longer than they expected, no marvel if the faith of the world about Christ's coming is fled and gone long ago, yea, and that the children also are put to it to wait, since a scripture 'little while' doth prove so long. For that which the apostle saith, 'yet a little while,' doth prove to some to be a very long little.[2]

True, Zacharias had then to do with angels, and that made him stay so long. O but Jesus is with God, before him, in his presence, talking with him, swallowed up in him, and with his glory, and that is one cause he stays so long. He is there also pleading his blood for his tempted ones, and interceding for all his elect, and waits there till all his be fitted for, and ready to enter into glory. I say, he is there, and there must be till then; and this is another reason why he doth stay the time we count so long.

And, indeed, it is a wonder to me, that Jesus Christ our Lord should once think, now he is there, of returning hither again, considering the ill treatment he met with here before. But what will not love do? Surely he would never touch the ground again, had he not a people here that cannot be made perfect but by his coming to them. He also is made judge of quick and dead, and will get him glory in the ruin of them that hate him.

His people are as himself to him. Can a loving husband abide to be always from a beloved spouse? Besides, as I said, he is to pay the wicked off, for all their wickedness, and that in that very plat where they have committed it. Wherefore the day appointed for this is set, and he will, and shall come quickly to do it. For however the time may seem long to us, yet, according to the reckoning of God, it is but a little while since he went into the holiest to intercede. 'A thousand years with the Lord is as one day;' and after this manner of counting, he has not been gone yet full two days into the holiest. 'The Lord is not slack concerning his promise, as some men count slackness;' 'he will come quickly, and will not tarry.'[3]

---

[1] 2 Peter 3:4.
[2] John 16:16; Hebrews 10:37.
[3] 2 Peter 3; Hebrews 10:37.

LXIX. OF THE CHERUBIMS, AND OF THEIR BEING PLACED OVER THE MERCY-SEAT IN THE INNER TEMPLE.

THERE were also cherubims in the most holy place, which were set on high above the mercy-seat.[1]

1. These are called by the apostles, 'the cherubims of glory shadowing the mercy-seat.'[2]

2. These cherubims were figures of the angels of God, as in other places we have proved.

3. It is said these cherubims were made of image work, and that in such manner, as that they could, as some think, move their wings by art; wherefore it is said, 'they stretched forth their wings;' the wings of the 'cherubims spread themselves;' and that the 'cherubims spread forth *their* wings over the place of the ark, . . . and the staves thereof above.'[3]

4. I read also of these cherubims, that they had chariots and wheels; by which is taught us how ready and willing the angels are to fetch us when commanded, unto the paradise of God; for these chariots were types of the bosoms of the angels; and these wheels, of the quickness of their motion to come for us when sent. 'The chariots of God *are* twenty thousand, *even* thousands of angels; the Lord *is* among them, *as in* Sinai, in the holy *place*.'[4]

5. What difference, if any, there is between cherubims and seraphims, into that I shall not now inquire; though I believe that there are diverse orders and degrees of angels in the heavens, as there are degrees and diverse orders among men in the world. But that these cherubims were figures of the holy angels, their being thus placed in the holy oracle doth declare; for their dwelling-place is heaven, though they, for our sakes, are conversant in the world.[5]

6. It is said that these cherubims, in this holy place, did stand upon their feet, to show, 1. That the angels of heaven are not fallen from their station, as the other angels are. 2. To show also that they are always ready, at God's bidding, to run with swift-ness to do his pleasure. 3. To show also that they shall continue

---

[1] 1 Kings 6:23–28.

[2] Hebrews 9:5.

[3] 1 Kings 6:27; 2 Chronicles 3:13; 5:8.

[4] 1 Chronicles 28:18; Ezekiel 10:9, 15–16, 18–20; 2 Kings 6:17; Psalm 68:17; 2 Kings 2:11; Daniel 9:2.

[5] Hebrews 1.

in their station, being therein confirmed by Jesus Christ, 'by whom all things consist.'[1]

7. It is said 'their faces *were* inward,' looking one to another, yet withal somewhat ascending, to show that the angels both behold and wonder at the mysteries of grace, as it is displayed to usward from off the mercy-seat. The faces of the cherubims 'shall *look* one to another; towards the mercy-seat shall the faces of the cherubims be.'[2]

(1.) 'Towards the mercy-seat.' They are desirous to see it, and how from hence, I say, mercy doth look towards us.

(2.) 'They look one towards another,' to show that they agree to rejoice in the salvation of our souls.[3]

(3.) They are said to stand above the mercy-seat, perhaps to show that the angels have not need of those acts of mercy and forgiveness as we have, who stand below, and are sinners. They stand above it; they are holy. I do not say they have no need that the goodness of God should be extended to them, for it is by that they have been and are preserved; but they need not to be forgiven, for they have committed no iniquity.

(4.) They stand there also with wings stretched out, to show how ready, if need be, the angels are to come from heaven to preach this gospel to the world.[4]

(5.) It is said in this, that thus standing, their wings did reach from wall to wall; from one side of this holy house to the other; to show that all the angels within the boundaries of the heavens, with one consent and one mind, are ready to come down to help and serve, and do for God's elect at his command.

It is said, also, that their wings are stretched on high, to show that they are only delighted in those duties which are enjoined them by the high and lofty One, and not inclined, no not to serve the saints in their sensual or fleshly designs. It may be also to show that they are willing to take their flight from one end of heaven to the other, to serve God and his church for good.[5]

---

[1] Colossians 1:17.

[2] Exodus 25:20; 2 Chronicles 3:13; 1 Peter 1:12; Ephesians 3:10.

[3] Luke 15:10.

[4] Luke 2:9–14.

[5] Matthew 13:41, 49; 24:31; 25:31; 2 Thessalonians 1:7–8.

LXX. OF THE FIGURES THAT WERE UPON
THE WALLS OF THE INNER TEMPLE.

THE wall of the inner temple, which was a type of heaven, was, as I have already told you, ceiled with cedar from the bottom to the top. Now by the vision of Ezekiel, it is said this wall was carved with cherubims and palm trees. 'So that a palm tree *was* between a cherub and a cherub, and *every* cherub had two faces; so that the face of a man *was* toward the palm tree on the one side, and the face of a young lion toward the palm tree on the other side. *It was* made through all the house round about; from the ground unto above the door *were* cherubims and palm trees made.'[1]

1. As to these cherubims and palm trees, I have already told you what I think them to be figures of. The cherubims are figures of the holy angels, and the palm trees of upright ones; we therefore here are to discourse only of the placing of them in the heavens.

2. Now you see the palm trees in the holiest are placed between a cherub and a cherub, round about the house, which methinks should be to signify that the saints shall not there live by faith and hope, as here, but in the immediate enjoyment of God; for to be placed between the cherubims, is to be placed where God dwells; for Holy Writ says plainly, He dwells between the cherubims, even where here it is said these palm trees, or upright ones are placed.[2] The church on earth is called God's house, and he will dwell in it for ever; and heaven itself is called God's house, and we shall dwell in it for ever, and that between the cherubims. This is more than grace, this is grace and glory, glory indeed.

3. To dwell between the cherubims may be also to show that there we shall be equal to the angels. Mark, here is a palm tree and a cherub, a palm tree and a cherub. Here we are a little lower, but there we shall not be a whit behind the very chief of them. A palm tree and a cherub, an upright one between the cherubs, will then be round about the house; we shall be placed in the same rank; 'neither can they die any more, for they are equal unto the angels.'[3]

4. The palm trees thus placed, may be also to show us that the elect of God shall there take up the vacancies of the fallen

---

[1] Ezekiel 41:18–20.

[2] 1 Samuel 4:4; 2 Kings 19:15; 1 Chronicles 13:6; Psalm 80:1; Isaiah 37:16.

[3] Luke 20:36.

angels; they for sin were cast down from the holy heavens, and we by grace shall be caught up thither, and be placed between a cherub and a cherub. When I say their places, I do not mean the fickleness of that state, that they for want of electing love did stand in while in glory; for the heavens, by the blood of Christ, is now to us become a purchased possession; wherefore, as we shall have their place in the heavenly kingdom, so, by virtue of redeeming blood, we shall there abide, and go no more out; for by that means that kingdom will stand to us unshaken.[1]

5. These palm trees, I say, seem to take their places who for sin were cast from thence. The elect therefore take that place in possession, but a better crown for ever. Thus 'Israel possessed that of the Canaanites;' and David, Saul's kingdom; and Matthias, the place, the apostleship of Judas.[2]

6. Nor were the habitations which the fallen angels lost, excepting that which was excepted before, at all inferior to theirs that stood; for their captain and prince is called son of the morning, for he was the antitype there.[3]

7. Thus, you see, they were placed from the ground up to above the door; that is, from the lowest to the highest angel there. For as there are great saints and small ones in the church on earth, so there are angels of divers degrees in heaven, some greater than some; but the smallest saint, when he gets to heaven, shall have an angel's dignity, an angel's place. From the ground you find a palm tree between a cherub and a cherub.

8. And every cherub had two faces—so here; but I read in Ezekiel 10:14, that they had four faces apiece. The first was the face of a cherubim; the second, the face of a man; the third, the face of a lion; and the fourth, the face of an eagle.

9. They had two faces apiece; not to show that they were of a double heart, for 'their appearances and themselves' were the same, and 'they went every one straight forward.'[4] These two faces, then, were to show here the quickness of their apprehension, and their terribleness to execute the mind of God. The face of a man signifies them masters of reason; the face of a lion, the terribleness of their presence.[5]

---

[1] Hebrews 9:12; 12:22–24, 28; Revelation 3:12.
[2] Acts 1:20–26.
[3] Isaiah 14:12.
[4] Ezekiel 10:22.
[5] 1 Corinthians 13:12; Judges 13:6.

In another place I read of their wheels; yea, that themselves, 'their whole bodies, and their backs, and their hands, and their wings, and the wheels *were* full of eyes round about.'[1] And this is to show us how knowing and quick-sighted they are in all providences and dark dispensations, and how nimble in apprehending the mischievous designs of the enemies of God's church, and so how able they are to undermine them. And forasmuch also as they have the face of a lion, we by that are showed how full of power they are to kill and to destroy, when God says, Go forth and do so. Now, with these we must dwell and cohabit, a palm tree and a cherub; a palm tree and a cherub must be from the ground to above the door, round about the house—the heavens.

'So that the face of a man *was* toward the palm tree on the one side, and the face of a young lion toward the palm tree on the other side.' By these two faces may be also showed that we in the heavens shall have glory sufficient to familiarize us to the angels. Their lion-like looks, with which they used to fright the biggest saint on earth, as you have it,[2] shall then be accompanied with the familiar looks of a man. Then angels and men shall be fellows, and have to do with each as such.

Thus you see something of that little that I have found in the temple of God.

---

[1] Ezekiel 1:18; 10:12.
[2] Genesis 32:30; Judges 13:15, 22.

Made in the USA
Las Vegas, NV
22 October 2023

79486827R00080